QlikView for Finance

Deliver dynamic business intelligence dashboards for financial analysis with QlikView

B. Diane Blackwood

BIRMINGHAM - MUMBAI

QlikView for Finance

First published: September 2015

Production reference: 1230915

Published by Packt Publishing Ltd.
Livery Place
35 Livery Street
Birmingham B3 2PB, UK.

ISBN 978-1-78439-574-2

www.packtpub.com

Credits

Author
B. Diane Blackwood

Reviewers
Sokkorn Cheav
Deepak Vadithala
Alan J Watt

Acquisition Editor
Harsha Bharwani

Content Development Editor
Siddhesh Salvi

Technical Editor
Siddhesh Patil

Copy Editor
Sarang Chari

Project Coordinator
Kranti Berde

Proofreader
Safis Editing

Indexer
Mariammal Chettiyar

Graphics
Disha Haria

Production Coordinator
Nilesh R. Mohite

Cover Work
Nilesh R. Mohite

Disclaimer

QlikTech, QlikView, Qlik, Q, Qlik Sense, and other QlikTech products and services as well as their respective logos are trademarks or registered trademarks of QlikTech International AB.[VP1]

About the Author

B. Diane Blackwood has worked as a consultant implementing business intelligence and corporate performance management solutions since 2005. She has extensive experience in multiple industries—from microelectronics to heavy equipment manufacturing, medical, legal, and retail—using software to implement BI and CPM solutions. Diane currently works for Strafford Technology, LLC creating a data warehouse using SQL Server 2012. In 2010, she worked for El Camino Hospital, where she created a data warehouse and data marts to feed QlikView. Diane and her husband, Bob, moved from Chicago to Albuquerque in June, 2012.

She wrote a QlikView recipe book entitled *Instant QlikView 11 Application Development* for Packt Publishing in 2013. Diane has also written biographical encyclopedia articles on several known personalities, including Charles Babbage, Erving Goffman, and Isaac Asimov.

About the Reviewers

Sokkorn Cheav was a .Net developer, creating Windows applications and working on Crystal Reports for ten years, until he was shown a QlikView demo, a very powerful Business Intelligence tool. Soon after this revelation, he started working with this new tool, focusing entirely on QlikView and delivering BI solutions. Sokkorn spends the majority of his time creating QlikView applications, managing servers, and running projects in the fields of MNC, services, microfinance, power plan, and hospitality.

In April 2012, he won the first place in the QlikView Mobile App contest, which was ranked top in the chart. This competition was hosted by QlikTech and had more than 1,400 participants. There, Sokkorn's fantastic app was selected by popular vote and judged to be the best on many criteria by QlikTech.

He is active on the Qlik Community and other social media sites where he shares his enthusiasm for QlikView with other users and helps them as well.

I would like to thank my mother, Heng Pann; my father, Lak Cheav; my elder brother, Sokun Cheav; my elder sister, Sokkeang Cheav; my sister, Sokkim Cheav; my youngest sister, Sokngim Cheav; and my wife, Angkeakeo Hak for their understanding and support through all the projects and endeavors that I undertake.

Deepak Vadithala is a Qlik architect and Qlik Luminary for the year 2014 who has been building BI/Qlik applications since 2005. He has worked on many successful QlikView and SQL Server implementations, right from their inception though implementation and deployment. Deepak's experience and skills range from application development and UI design to system administration. He also has experience working in the investment banking, retail, media, advertising, and research sectors.

Deepak holds the QlikView Designer, Developer and Administrator certifications. He is currently focusing on Apache Pig, Apache Hive, and D3.

Deepak shares his tips and tricks on Qlik products on www.qlikshare.com. You can also follow him on Twitter at @dvadithala, where he tweets about technology.

Alan J Watt has a broad range of system development and management skills gained from over 30 years of experience in the IT industry. These include business and systems analysis and application design and development through team and project management to IT management. He has experience in selling (creating presale demos), developing, and implementing software applications for different industries, such as finance, distribution, manufacturing, customer service, planned maintenance, and warehousing.

Alan is a certified QlikView developer with 5 years of experience in working with QlikView customers. He also has strong skills in working with JDEdwards (due to over 16 years of experience) and has been developing with Visual Basic for over 12 years.

Alan enjoys spending time with his wife and five kids and has many personal interests, such as football, karate, tai chi, bird watching, and cooking. He is an avid reader of literature related to sci-fi, computer technology, and environmental issues.

www.PacktPub.com

Support files, eBooks, discount offers, and more

For support files and downloads related to your book, please visit www.PacktPub.com.

Did you know that Packt offers eBook versions of every book published, with PDF and ePub files available? You can upgrade to the eBook version at www.PacktPub.com and, as a print book customer, you are entitled to a discount on the eBook copy. Get in touch with us at service@packtpub.com for more details.

At www.PacktPub.com, you can also read a collection of free technical articles, sign up for a range of free newsletters, and receive exclusive discounts and offers on Packt books and eBooks.

https://www2.packtpub.com/books/subscription/packtlib

Do you need instant solutions to your IT questions? PacktLib is Packt's online digital book library. Here, you can search, access, and read Packt's entire library of books.

Why subscribe?

- Fully searchable across every book published by Packt
- Copy-and-paste, print, and bookmark content
- On-demand and accessible via a Web browser

Free access for Packt account holders

If you have an account with Packt at www.PacktPub.com, you can use this to access PacktLib today and view nine entirely free books. Simply use your login credentials for immediate access.

Instant updates on new Packt books

Get notified! Find out when new books are published by following @PacktEnterprise on Twitter or the *Packt Enterprise* Facebook page.

Table of Contents

Preface

QlikView is a business intelligence (BI) platform that enables the creation of dynamic applications for the analysis of financial data. QlikView is based on an in-memory data store, which means that BI applications can refresh data in real time. This book will lead the finance professional through the use of Qlikview for data analysis and visualization in finance, where it is used extensively. It therefore assumes that the reader has a good knowledge of finance.

This book illustrates the QlikView financial key performance indicators and discusses planning and analysis, expense management, inventory tracking, and the do's and don'ts of information display. After reading this book, you will be able to create your own financial key performance indicators and analyze how demonstration KPIs, charts, and tables are created in the existing QlikView example applications.

What this book covers

Chapter 1, *Getting That Financial Data into QlikView*, discusses how to obtain and install QlikView, create our first QlikView analysis, and add data to that analysis. Here, we will scratch the surface of the things that can be done with QlikView.

Chapter 2, *QlikView Dashboard Financial KPIs*, answers question such as: What are Key Performance Indicators (KPIs)? How can we display the sales from our sample data as KPIs? How do we create our first thermometer-type gauge? Here, we will discuss the three most common financial KPIs and how to put them in a QlikView dashboard. You will also learn how you can use QlikView to extend your revenue ratio reporting.

Chapter 3, KPIs in the Financial Officer QlikView Dashboard, will illustrate the KPI tab with the example of a CFO dashboard in detail. You will discover which objects are used on the sheet and how they are layered to create a specific design look. Also, you will find out how to use the inline wizard to produce specific display results. You will learn how to set up actions within a text object. You will be able to use variables to make a chart visible or invisible and examine how a chart object can contain more than one chart.

Chapter 4, QlikView Asset Management with Multiple Data Sources, discusses the most important thing about asset management: being able to obtain and merge data from multiple sources. This chapter is an introduction to data loading options with various data sources.

Chapter 5, QlikView Sales Analysis, discusses analyzing an existing dashboard to learn the good and bad practices in dashboard design. It takes a look at creating a Group button to make more data available on a single display without overcrowding, and creating our own Sales Analysis dashboard tab, including our own containers and other sheet objects.

Chapter 6, QlikView Forecasting and Trends, continues with the Sales Analysis dashboard, adding trending lines and forecasting out to three months. Following this exercise, we will examine the Trending dashboard and how it is assembled. We will choose colors and apply them, adding them to our own theme. We will create an Input Box and apply the input data to a formula in the What If? dashboard example.

Chapter 7, QlikView Inventory Analysis, illustrates the use of the Inventory tab in a sample CFO dashboard to get ideas for inventory tracking and management. We will examine a four-quadrant layout, intuitive controls and the KPI, inventory turnover. You will be introduced to pivot tables and the additional drill-down navigation analysis features offered by them.

Chapter 8, QlikView Order Details Dashboard, examines supply chain analysis options using the Order Details tab of the dashboard in the CFO example and compares the tab to the online demonstration titled Order and Inventory Management. We will create a Fast Change type for an existing straight table, export data to Excel, color-code the data, set our own number formats, and create a dynamic expression.

Chapter 9, QlikView Expenses Dashboard, introduces the analysis of another four-quadrant dashboard layout to explain the usefulness of the display options. We will switch a sheet object so that it can be minimized and maximized. We will also review standard formula, including column variances, and experiment with pivot table formatting. Finally, we will create a URL link in an existing pivot table, and learn how to bundle images.

Chapter 10, Sharing Your QlikView Insights, signposts the next steps you can take (now that you have mastered using QlikView to provide financial management insights) to share the new information with business colleagues who need it.

What you need for this book

Two sample data Excel spreadsheets used in *Chapter 1, Getting That Financial Data into QlikView* and *Chapter 2, QlikView Dashboard Financial KPIs* are available for download from your account at `http://www.PacktPub.com`. Their names are CHData_Oct.xls and CHData-Nov.xls.

Two additional sample data Excel spreadsheets are available for download from your account at `http://www.PacktPub.com`, both used in *Chapter 2, QlikView Dashboard Financial KPIs*. One is named Target.xls and the other is named IS3yr.xls.

Two images and an Excel spreadsheet are available for download from your account at `http://ww.PacktPub.com`. They are used in *Chapter 9, QlikView Expenses Dashboard*. The spreadsheet is named MonthImages.xls and the image files are Gecko.jpg and Fish.jpg.

Who this book is for

This book will teach the finance professional how to use QlikView for data analysis and visualization in finance. It assumes, therefore, that users have a good knowledge of finance and are interested in learning more about financial analysis and dashboard options. QlikView is instrumental in facilitating such analyses.

Conventions

In this book, you will find a number of styles of text that distinguish between different kinds of information. Here are some examples of these styles, and an explanation of their meaning.

Code words in paragraph are shown as "The filenames are `CHData-Oct.xls` and `CHData-Nov.xls`".

Code words shown in the QlikView interfaces are shown in text as follows:

```
SET DateFormat='M/D/YYYY';
SET TimestampFormat='M/D/YYYY h:mm:ss[.fff] TT';
SET MonthNames='Jan;Feb;Mar;Apr;May;Jun;Jul;Aug;Sep;Oct;Nov;Dec';
SET DayNames='Mon;Tue;Wed;Thu;Fri;Sat;Sun';

LOAD Company,
     [AcctGroup],
     [Account-Name],
     Count,
     Unit.,
     Acct.5,
     Acct.6,
     Nature,
     CostCenter,
     Month,
     Year,
     Amount
FROM
[C:\Users\User\Documents\My Docs\Packt Publishing\QlikView Finance
Book\QVFA Chapter 1\CHData-OCT.xlsx]
(ooxml, embedded labels);
```

New terms and **important words** are shown in bold. Words that you see on the screen, in menus or dialog boxes for example, appear in the text like this: "Click on **Download Now**, and select your preferred **Language**".

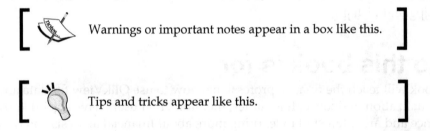

Warnings or important notes appear in a box like this.

Tips and tricks appear like this.

Reader feedback

Feedback from our readers is always welcome. Let us know what you think about this book—what you liked or may have disliked. Reader feedback is important for us to develop titles that you really get the most out of.

To send us general feedback, simply send an e-mail to feedback@packtpub.com, and mention the book title through the subject of your message.

If there is a topic that you have expertise in and you are interested in either writing or contributing to a book, see our author guide on www.packtpub.com/authors.

Customer support

Now that you are the proud owner of a Packt book, we have a number of things to help you to get the most from your purchase.

Downloading the example code

You can download the example code files for all Packt books you have purchased from your account at http://www.packtpub.com. If you purchased this book elsewhere, you can visit http://www.packtpub.com/support and register to have the files e-mailed directly to you.

Errata

Although we have taken every care to ensure the accuracy of our content, mistakes do happen. If you find a mistake in one of our books—maybe a mistake in the text or the code—we would be grateful if you would report this to us. By doing so, you can save other readers from frustration and help us improve subsequent versions of this book. If you find any errata, please report them by visiting http://www.packtpub.com/support, selecting your book, clicking on the **errata submission form** link, and entering the details of your errata. Once your errata are verified, your submission will be accepted and the errata will be uploaded to our website, or added to any list of existing errata, under the Errata section of that title.

Piracy

Piracy of copyright material on the Internet is an ongoing problem across all media. At Packt, we take the protection of our copyright and licenses very seriously. If you come across any illegal copies of our works, in any form, on the Internet, please provide us with the location address or website name immediately so that we can pursue a remedy.

Please contact us at copyright@packtpub.com with a link to the suspected pirated material.

We appreciate your help in protecting our authors, and our ability to bring you valuable content.

Questions

You can contact us at questions@packtpub.com if you are having a problem with any aspect of the book, and we will do our best to address it.

1
Getting That Financial Data into QlikView

QlikView is an easy-to-use business intelligence product. It is designed to facilitate ad hoc relationship analysis but can also be used for more formal corporate performance applications for the financial user. It is designed to use a methodology of *direct discovery* to analyze data from multiple sources. QlikView is designed to allow you to do your own business discovery and to take you quickly out of the data management stage and into the data relationship investigation stage. Investigating relationships and outliers in financial data more quickly can lead to better management.

In this chapter, we will cover the following topics:

- When do we use QlikView?
- Getting ready — downloading and installing QlikView
- Becoming familiar with QlikView
    - Opening and examining QlikView
    - Loading data from Excel
- How QlikView works for analysis — finding the out of balance
- Modifying the load script
    - Loading more than one spreadsheet
    - Automatically linking data

When do we use QlikView?

With that in mind, when would you want to use QlikView? You would use it when you wish to analyze and quickly see trends and exceptions that—with normal financial application-oriented BI products—would not be readily apparent without days of setting up by consultants and technology departments. With QlikView, you can also analyze data relationships that are not measured in monetary units. Certainly, QlikView can be used to analyze sales trends and stock performance, but other relationships soon become apparent when using QlikView.

This chapter will take you through getting financial ledger data into QlikView and analyzing the out of balance.

Downloading and installing QlikView

QlikView is available in a free, personal edition from the QlikTech company website at http://www.qlik.com. The version of QlikView used in the screenshots in this book is *11.20.12577.0 64 bit*.

If you have never downloaded your own personal edition of QlikView before or you want the latest edition, navigate to the website and click on the button labeled **Free Download**. Scroll down to, where you will be asked to register and choose a username.

Click on **Download Now**, and select your preferred **Language** and the version of the product you need for your environment. Choose the correct version for your computer.

Click on the **Download QlikView Now** button, and when your system asks you what you want to do, click on the **Run** button. You may want to come back and download the tutorial too.

Follow the instructions on the install screens. Give your system permission to install the software, if necessary, and accept the license agreement. It can take 10–20 minutes to download and install depending on your Internet speed. The latest version of QlikView is now available to use.

 There are two sample data Excel spreadsheets (available for download from your account at http://www.PacktPub.com) that are used in the first chapter. Their names are CHData_Oct.xls and CHData-Nov.xls.

Becoming familiar with QlikView

This book is designed to give financial executives and personnel a greater understanding of how to use QlikView for financial insight. The lessons and examples in this book presume that you have already downloaded QlikView and can start it from your program menu. You should also have a working knowledge of Microsoft Excel.

Opening and examining QlikView

Start QlikView from your **Start** program menu in Windows. After QlikView starts, you can begin to navigate around in it and start to familiarize yourself with the environment.

QlikView consists of two parts: the *sheet* contains sheet objects, such as charts or list boxes that show clickable information, and the *load script* stores information about the data and the data sources that the data is coming from.

Financial professionals always use Excel to examine their data. So, we are going to start by loading data from an Excel sheet using the **New** document button. QlikView can also help you create a basic document sheet containing a chart. The newest version of QlikView comes with sample *Sales Order* data that can be used to investigate and create sheet objects.

To use data from other file types, you can use `File Wizard: Type` that you start from the **Edit Script** dialog by clicking on the **Table Files** button.

Using the **Edit Script** dialog, you can view your data script, edit the script, and add other data sources. You reload your data by clicking on the **Reload** button. If you just want to analyze data from an existing QlikView file and analyze the information in it, you do not need to work with the script at all.

After QlikView opens, you will see the default start screen:

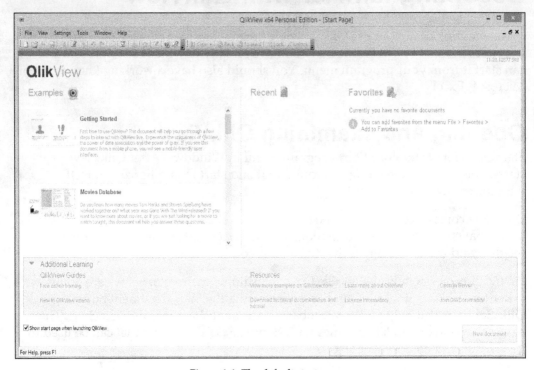

Figure 1-1: The default start screen

Here, you will see the side menu with **Getting Started** ▶ as the highlighted selection; along with **Recent**, which will be blank the first time QlikView is opened; **Favorites**, which is also empty at this point; **Open in Server**, which allows you to register the QlikView server if your company has an Enterprise QlikView license and is running QlikView from a server; and **Resources**, where you can follow links back to the QlikView website and see more examples. In the lower-left corner, you have the option to uncheck the box to show this screen when starting QlikView. Leave that option checked to make it easy to navigate to examples and training.

Getting Started shows that you are running *QlikView Personal Edition*, with options to use **Learn QlikView** and to see **Examples**. The third entry, under **Examples** in this version, is **Data Visualization**, which is a very good tutorial on what types of charts to use to aid in visual discovery and understanding of your data relationships.

Loading data from Excel

Now, let's create our first QlikView document by loading data from Excel. Start by clicking on the **New Document** button located in the lower-right corner of this version of QlikView. Prior editions of the personal download have other options, such as a link under **Learn QlikView** saying **Create a new QlikView document by loading data from an Excel file**.

For this example, we will use sample financial data downloaded from an ERP system into Excel. This sample data can be downloaded from your account at Packt Publishing at http://www.PacktPub.com. The filenames are CHData-Oct.xls and CHData-Nov.xls. Review the data in Excel before you load it to learn how a load file should be set up.

There are six steps to setting up the load file:

1. Select the data source. Do this by clicking on **Browse** and navigating to the Excel file that you are going to analyze. First, we will load the file named CHData-Oct.xls.

2. Verify the data and choose to use column headers from this data file (or create your own for each column in the data). With the sample data, we will use the existing column headers.

3. Save your new QlikView QVW file and give it a name of your choice. Our example uses CheyenneCO.qvw.

4. Choose the chart type that you wish to create for your first sheet object. Here, because it is one month of financial type data, we will choose a bar chart to start examining our sample data.

5. Select the dimension(s) that you want to use in your first chart. Here, we selected **AcctGroup**. We can alternatively choose **CostCenter**. **Dimensions** represents the columns of data from the Excel file that we loaded. We will add a mathematical expression, such as sum or average. We will just add the sum expression of the **Amount** column we loaded.

6. For our final selections, we will choose a table box that will list and group all our fields.

We have now created our first QlikView application. Move your objects around so that your table box is lower in the screen, and widen it so that all the columns can be seen. Then, in the free space above, right-click and add a statistics box. I have named it **Statistics Box** in the screenshot. Make sure that you choose **Amount** as your statistic. If you prefer, you can remove or add statistical measures from your statistics. Your *QlikView Financial Analysis of Cheyenne Company* should appear similar to the following screenshot:

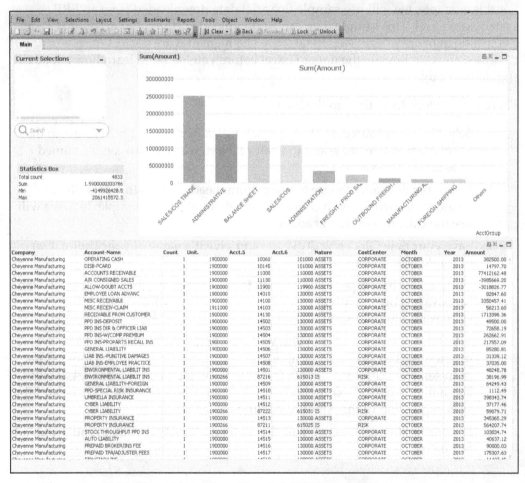

Figure 1-2: Our financial analysis QlikView application

How QlikView works for analysis – finding the out of balance

As you can see in the menu drop-down, there are multiple sheet object types to choose from, such as **List Box**, **Statistics Box**, **Chart**, **Input Box**, **Current Selections Box**, **Multi Box**, **Table Box**, **Button**, **Text Object**, **Line/Arrow Object**, **Slider/Calendar Object**, and **Bookmark Object**. We will cover more of them in the course of this book. **Help** and **Extended Examples** on the QlikView website will allow you to explore ideas beyond the scope of this book.

 Help on any item can be obtained by using the **Help** menu in the top **Menu** bar.

We chose the **Statistic Box** Sheet object to add the grand total to our analysis. From this, we can see that the total company is out of balance by **$1.59**. From an auditor's point of view, this amount is probably small enough to be immaterial, but, from our point of view as financial professionals, we want to know where our books are not in balance.

To make our investigation easier, we will add one additional sheet object—**List Box**—for **Company**. Right-click and, from the **Context** menu, choose **New Sheet Object**; then choose **List Box**. We will now go through each tab of the **List Box** properties.

On the **General** tab of **List Box**, we will give the new **List Box** the **Title** of Company List. The object ID will be system-generated. We choose the **Field Company** from the fields available in the data file that we loaded. We can check the box to show **Frequency** in **Percent** below **Title** and **Field**, which will only tell us how many account lines in **October** were loaded for each company.

In the **Expressions** tab, we can add formulas to analyze the data. Here, we will click on **ADD** and will choose **SUM**; since we only have numerical data in the **Amount** field, we will sum **Amount**. Don't forget to click on the **PASTE** button to move your expression into **Expression Checker**. **Expression Checker** will tell you whether the expression format is OK or whether there is a syntax problem.

 If you forget to move your expression into **Expression Checker** with the **PASTE** button, the expression will not be saved and will not appear in your application.

The **Sort** tab allows you to change the **Sort** criteria from text to numeric or even date. We will not change the **Sort** for **Company**.

The **Presentation** tab allows you to adjust things such as column or row header wrap, cell borders, and background pictures.

The **Number** tab allows you to override the default format to tell the sheet whether you want to format the data as money, a percentage, or dates, for example. But in this version, it does not seem to be working properly until selected. We can use this tab on our table box that is currently labeled **Sum(Amount)** to format **Amount** as money after we have finished creating our new company **List Box**.

The **Font** tab lets you choose the display font you want to use, the display size, and whether to make your font bold.

Layout allows you to establish and apply themes and format the appearance of the sheet object, which, in this case, is **List Box**.

The **Caption** tab further formats the sheet object and allows us, in the case of **List Box**, to choose the icons that will appear in the top bar of the **List Box** so that we can use those icons to **Select** and **Clear** selections in the **List Box**. In this example, we have selected **Search**, **Select All**, and **Clear**. The following screenshot shows this:

Company	
American Distribution	0.00
Cheyenne Co L.P.	1.59
Cheyenne Holding	0.33
Cheyenne Manufacturing	0.00
Cheyenne National Inc	-0.33
Eliminations	0.00
Pioneer Payroll	0.00
Provo	0.00
Sales Corp	0.00
Warranty Care Corporation	0.00
Wheatland	0.00

Figure 1-3: Added company list box

We can now see that we are actually out of balance in three companies. **Cheyenne Co L.P.** is the company that is out of balance by **$1.59**, but **Cheyenne Holding** and **Cheyenne National Inc** seem to have balancing entries that balance at the total companies level but don't balance at the individual company level.

Now we need to edit our **Table Box** sheet object with the **Amount** displayed. Right-click on **the Straight Table** sheet object and choose **Properties** from the pop-up menu. In the first tab, the **General** tab, give **Table** a suitable name if desired. Then move over to the **Number** tab and choose **Money** for the number format. Click on **APPLY** to immediately apply the number format, and click on **OK** to close the wizard.

Now our **Straight Table** sheet object looks like the previous screenshot displaying dollar signs and two decimals for **Amount**.

We can analyze our data just using the list boxes by selecting **Company**, seeing which **Account Groups** are included, and seeing which **Cost Centers** are included (white) and which are excluded (gray). Our selected company shows up in green and in **Current Selection Box**.

By selecting **Cheyenne Holding**, we can see that it is indeed a holding company and doesn't have any manufacturing or sales accounting groups or cost centers. Also, that particular company is in balance.

Adding more data – modifying the load script

Next we will use the second Excel spreadsheet available from your Packt account:

`CHData-Nov.xls.`

 There are two sample data Excel spreadsheets (available for download from your account at `http://www.PacktPub.com`) that are used in the first chapter. Their names are `CHData_Oct.xls` and `CHData-Nov.xls`.

Loading more than one spreadsheet

To load more than one spreadsheet or to load from a different data source, we must edit the load script. The **Edit Script** dialog is opened from the **File** menu or by clicking on the **Edit Script** symbol in the toolbar.

Figure 1-4: A closeup of the File menu showing Edit Script

From the **Edit Script** interface, we can modify and execute a script that connects the QlikView document to an ODBC data source (or to data files of different types) and also pulls in the data source information.

Our first script was generated automatically; but scripts can be typed manually, or automatically generated scripts can be modified. Complex script statements must, at least partially, be entered manually. The statements, expressions, functions, and so on available for the creation of scripts are described in the **QlikView Help: Script Syntax** and **Script Expressions**.

The **Edit Script** dialog uses autocomplete so, when you type, the program tries to predict what is required in the script without you having to type it completely. The predictions include words that are part of the script syntax. The script is also color-coded by syntax components. The **Edit Script** interface and behavior can be customized by choosing **Tools** and **Editor Preferences**.

At the top of the dialog, a menu bar, with various script-related commands, is found. The most frequently used commands also appear in the toolbar. In the toolbar, there is also a drop-down list for the tabs of the **Edit Script** wizard.

 Make sure your Excel column headers aren't named the same if you are going to use them as labels. If the columns are named the same, QlikView automatically tries to combine them!

Once we have clicked on the **Edit Script** menu item, we will see the following script in the script interface:

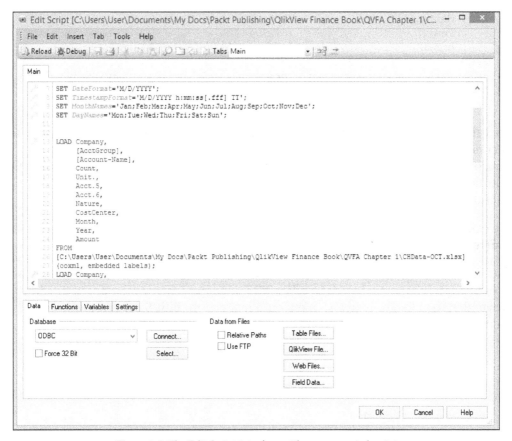

Figure 1-5: The Edit Script interface with our generated script

The script in the **Edit Script** interface is the automatically generated one that was created by the wizard when we started this QlikView file. The automatically generated script picked up the column names from the Excel file and put in some default formatting scripting. The actual text of the script is as follows:

```
SET DateFormat='M/D/YYYY';
SET TimestampFormat='M/D/YYYY h:mm:ss[.fff] TT';
SET MonthNames='Jan;Feb;Mar;Apr;May;Jun;Jul;Aug;Sep;Oct;Nov;Dec';
SET DayNames='Mon;Tue;Wed;Thu;Fri;Sat;Sun';


LOAD Company,
     [AcctGroup],
     [Account-Name],
     Count,
     Unit.,
     Acct.5,
     Acct.6,
     Nature,
     CostCenter,
     Month,
     Year,
     Amount
FROM
[C:\Users\User\Documents\My Docs\Packt Publishing\QlikView Finance
Book\QVFA Chapter 1\CHData-OCT.xlsx]
(ooxml, embedded labels);
```

We can change our date formats, month names, day names, our thousands, and our decimal separators by changing them in the automatically generated formats. We can copy this part of the script into new blank scripts to get started. The language selection that we made during the initial installation of QlikView determines the defaults assigned to this portion of the script.

We can add data from multiple sources, such as ODBC links, additional Excel tables, sources from the Web, FTP, and even other QlikView files.

Our first Excel file, which we used to create the initial QlikView document, is already in our script. It happened to be October 2013 data, but what if we wanted to add November data to our analysis? We would just go into **Edit Script** from the **File** menu and then click on the script itself.

Make sure your cursor is at the bottom of the script after the first Excel file path and description. If you do not position your cursor where you want your additional script information to populate, you could generate your new script code in the middle of your existing script code. If you make a mistake, click on **CANCEL** and start over.

After navigating to the script location where you want to add your new code, click on the **Table Files** button below the script and toward the center-right—the first button in the column. Click on **NEXT** through the next four screens unless you need to add column labels or transform your data for analysis in some way. The following section is added to our script:

```
LOAD  Company,
      [AcctGroup],
      [Account-Name],
      Count,
      Unit.,
      Acct.5,
      Acct.6,
      Nature,
      CostCenter,
      Month,
      Year,
      Amount
FROM
[C:\Users\User\Documents\My Docs\Packt Publishing\QlikView Finance
Book\QVFA Chapter 1\CHData-NOV.xlsx]
(ooxml, embedded labels, table is LNData);
```

Comments can be added to scripts using // for a single line or by surrounding the comment by a beginning /* and an ending */; they show up in green. After using the **OK** button to get out of the **Edit Script interface**, there is another **File** menu item that can be used to see whether QlikView has correctly interpreted the joins. This is the **Table Viewer** menu item. You cannot edit in the **Table** view, but it is convenient to visualize how the table fields are interacting.

Tell the **Edit Script** interface OK by clicking on the **OK** button in the lower-right corner. This will save the changes to the script. Now, using the **File** menu, navigate below **Edit Script** to the **RELOAD** menu item, and click on that to reload your data. If you receive any error messages, the solutions can be researched in the QlikView **Help**. In this case, QlikView knew that we were adding data to the same table, the layout was the same, and the column names were the same. But looking at company **List Box** and **Amount Statistics Box**, we see everything added together. The following screenshot shows this:

Amount	
Total count	9468
Sum	$1.56
Average	0.00

Company	
American Distribution	0.00
Cheyenne Co L.P.	1.59
Cheyenne Holding	5591425.03
Cheyenne Manufacturing	0.00
Cheyenne National Group ...	0.00
Cheyenne National Inc	-0.33
Eliminations	-5591424.70
Pioneer Payroll	0.00
Provo	-0.03
Sales Corp	0.00
Warranty Care Corporation	0.00
Wheatland	0.00

Figure 1-6: Data doubled after the reload with the additional file

The reason why this is happening is that we do not have a selection to split the months and only select October or November or to split October from November. What do we do? Now that we have more than one month of data, we can add another **List Box** with **Months**. This will automatically link up with our **Chart** and **Straight Table** sheet objects to separate our monthly data.

First, we will add a new **List Box** for **Months**. Right-click on the sheet and select **New Sheet Object | List Box**. In the **General** tab, we will choose **Field** (labeled **Month** in the Excel files). Then, we go to the **Sort** tab and check **Sort by Text**. Finally, we choose the icons that we want to appear on the top bar of **List Box** in the **Captions** tab.

When we choose **OCTOBER** or **NOVEMBER**, our sheet objects automatically show the correct sum of the individual months. Your QlikView document will now look somewhat similar to this next screenshot, depending on how you arranged your added sheet objects:

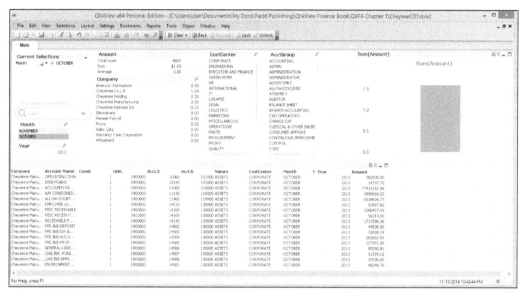

Figure 1-7: A QlikView document

Summary

You learned how to obtain and install QlikView. You created your first QlikView analysis and learned how to add data to that analysis. We have scratched the surface of some of the things that can be done with QlikView. The next chapters are designed to tackle ways of analyzing different financial information within QlikView.

2

QlikView Dashboard Financial KPIs

There are literally thousands of key performance indicators on http://www.kpilibrary.com. Many are the same, or very similar, formulas with different names, and every business concern's CEO and CFO have their own measure that helps them measure business performance in a way that is meaningful to them.

In this chapter, you will learn about the following concepts:

- What are key performance indicators (KPIs)?
  - ° Display sales as a KPI
  - ° Our first thermometer-type gauge

- What are the three most common financial KPIs?
  - ° How to create and display the KPIs: **Return on Investment (ROI)**, **Return on Assets (ROA)** and **Return on Expenses (ROE)** in a QlikView dashboard
  - ° Set expressions
  - ° Gauge displays

- How to use QlikView to extend your revenue ratio reporting
  - ° List Box sheet objects vs charts

- Common size income statement

What are key performance indicators?

Key performance indicators, also known as KPIs, are measurements used to judge how well your business is doing. They lend themselves well to use in visual displays, such as graphs, thermometers, charts, and gauges used in dashboards. A visual of a KPI in a dashboard should not be complicated, should not require elaborate explanation, nor should it be redundant to the actual numeric information.

Dashboards should display key information in a quick-to-digest format. Often, gauges, dials, and thermometers are used incorrectly, causing confusion rather than clarification. If you want to know more than the recommendations in the dashboard analyses in this book, suggested reading about good dashboard design is Stephen Few's *Information Dashboard Design*.

If we display the current sales in the current month, we hope that it will show a rising number daily. But just a number by itself might be meaningless to most of us. Are sales going up at a faster rate than average sales, sales during the same period last year, or expected or forecasted sales? A dashboard visual conveys that information without the need for elaborate text explanations. A dashboard visual of a specific KPI should allow the user to follow through to investigate more detailed information.

Display sales as a KPI

In our previously loaded sample data from *Chapter 1, Getting That Financial Data into QlikView*, sales is a grouping in the **AcctGroup** column and is a credit. It comes directly from the source system as a negative so that, when everything is summed up, we get a trial balance. That is why we could see the out of balances in our first tab. Sales will have to be multiplied by minus one (-1) in order for it to appear as a positive number. Also, we would like to have a target number to compare with **Sales**.

 There are two additional sample data Excel spreadsheets available for download from your account at http://www. PacktPub.com that are used in this chapter. One is named Target.xls and the other is named IS3yr.xls.

Our target is another Excel workbook named Target.xls that is available for download, or you can create your own workbook to load. The one available for download has this data:

Company	Target
Cheyenne Manufacturing	140000000
American Distribution	0

Company	Target
Cheyenne Holding	0
Sales Corp	1100000000
Wheatland	0
Pioneer Payroll	0
Provo	100000000
Cheyenne Co L.P.	450000000
Warranty Care Corporation	250000
Cheyenne National Inc	0
Eliminations	-908999539

To load `Target.xls`, choose **Edit Script** from the **File** menu. After navigating to the bottom of the existing script location where you want to add your new code, click on the **Table Files** button below the script and toward the center right; it is the first button in the column. Click on **NEXT** through the next four screens unless you need to add column labels or transform your data for analysis in some way. If you don't remember what this looks like or how to navigate, refer to *Chapter 1, Getting That Financial Data into QlikView*, for pictures.

Once we use **Edit** on the script to load the `Target` data, our script code looks similar to this:

```
LOAD Company,
    Target
FROM
[C:\Users\User\Documents\My Docs\Packt Publishing\QlikView Finance
Book\QVFA Chapter2\Target.xlsx]
(ooxml, embedded labels, table is Target);
```

Save your changes to the **Edit Script** interface by clicking on the **OK** button in the bottom-right corner. Now, using **File** menu, navigate below **Edit Script** to the **RELOAD** menu item, and click on that to reload your data.

Now, we will add a tab to our QlikView document by going to the **Layout** menu item and selecting **Add Sheet**. Rename this sheet to **Sales** by right-clicking on the sheet and choosing **Properties** from the menu.

Add the following sheet objects:

1. Right-click on the **Sales** tab sheet and choose **New Sheet Object**.

2. Add **Multi Box** with **Company**, **Month**, **Acct_Group**, **Nature**, and **Amount**.

3. Add three **List Box**, one each for **Company**, **Acct_Group**, and **Nature**.

Now, we will add a **Sales** thermometer-type gauge to our **Sales** tab.

Right-click on the **Sales** tab sheet, and choose **New Sheet Object,** as you did for **Multi Box.**

This time, choose **Charts,** and **Chart Wizard** will pop up. There are basically two types of gauges: the rectangular type, which are called thermometers because they tend to display data ratios in a horizontal or vertical format, and the ones called radio dial gauges because they display data in a circular format, such as the image on the QlikView **Gauge Chart** button.

These are the **Chart Wizard** tab steps related to making the thermometer-type gauge that we want to display for **Sales:**

1. On the **General** tab, enter your **Sales** object and select the **Gauge Chart** type by clicking on the button (number **5** in *Figure 1* of this chapter):

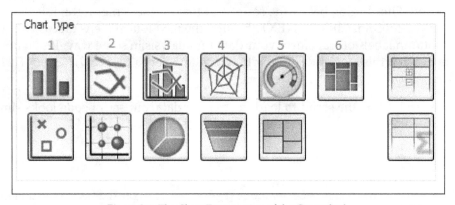

Figure 2-1: The Chart Type section of the General tab

2. Now, click on **NEXT.**

3. On the **Dimensions** tab, select **Company, AcctGroup, Amount,** and **Target** in the **Used Dimension** box.

4. Click on **NEXT.**

5. On the **Expressions** tab, enter the formula in **Expression Box** as it appears here:

    ```
    =(sum({$<AcctGroup={Sales}>} Amount) *(-1))
    ```

    Later in this chapter, the expression formulation will be explained.

6. Click on **OK,** and then click on **Add** to add another expression.

7. This time, use **Expression Builder** to input the following formula:

    ```
    =(sum(Target))
    ```

Do not forget to click on **Paste**, or else your expression will not move into the **Expression Box**.

8. Now, copy the Sum(Target) expression using *<Ctrl> C*.

9. Edit your first expression by adding a forward slash (/) and pasting the formula you copied using *<Ctrl > V* so that the formula now looks as shown here:

```
=(sum({$<AcctGroup={Sales}>} Amount) *(-1)) /(sum(Target))
```

10. Now, delete the second formula, =(sum(Target)), because we only created it to copy and paste into our first expression and to practice with the interface.

11. Click on **Next**.

12. Leave the **Sort** tab as it is and click on **Next**.

13. Select one of the rectangular gauge types, such as the bar with an indicator, from the **Style** tab, and change the orientation to horizontal if you prefer. It will look similar to the next screenshot:

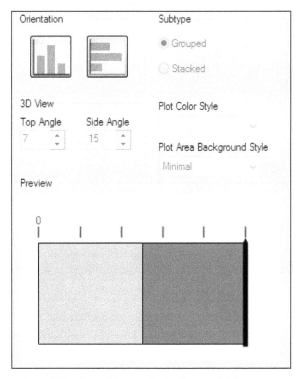

Figure 2-2: A bar with an indicator thermostat-type gauge

14. On the **Presentation** tab, perform the following steps:

    1. Change **Max** from **1** to **2**.

    2. Reverse the segments by promoting segment **2** above segment **1**.

    3. Add the text **Sales vs Target** to the **Text In Chart** box.

    4. Under **Show Scale**, change **Major Units** from **10** to **20**.

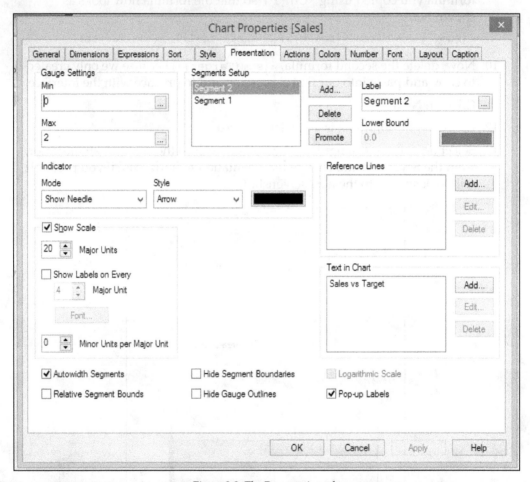

Figure 2-3: The Presentation tab

Because we have divided **Sales** by **Target**, we get a variance ratio. Use **Multi Box** to select **Company** with **Sales** over a month, and watch the indicator move and the ratio change.

Change your expression to the next formula to get the true variance percentage:

```
=((sum({$<AcctGroup={Sales}>} Amount) -(sum(Target)) ) *(-1)) /
(sum(Target))
```

Unfortunately, the formatting in this edition of gauge-type charts does not pick up percent formatting.

Also, recall that we don't have months in our `Target` numbers. If you would like to experiment, you can change your `Target` Excel spreadsheet. Add a column named **Month** and duplicate the company names. Make one each of **October** and **November** under the **Month** column and adjust your `Target` numbers.

What are the three most common financial KPIs?

The three most common financial KPIs used by financial analysts to evaluate a company's performance are Return on Assets (ROA), Return on Investment (ROI), and Return on Equity (ROE). They use these simple ratios because ratios enable them to compare small companies and large companies on an equal footing to determine whether to recommend buying stock in the company, loaning money to the company, or investing in the company in some other manner.

The standard calculation for these ratios is as follows:

1. Return on Assets (ROA)	NET INCOME / TOTAL ASSETS
2. Return on Investments (ROI)	NET INCOME / Long Term Liabilities + Equity
3. Return on Equity (ROE)	NET INCOME / Shareholder Equity

Adding ROI, ROA, and ROE into a QlikView dashboard

In order to create these ratios (ROA, ROI, and ROE) in QlikView, we need to use set analysis expressions. The basic format of a set analysis expression looks similar to this:

```
sum([{set_expression}][ and other related expressions  ])
```

The set expression is usually aggregated and can be modified by commands, such as [distinct], [total], specifying fields, or other expressions. Aggregation functions, such as Sum or Average, by default, aggregate over the current selection in your QlikView document, so the other options shown can be used to modify that behavior. For our ratios, we want to define other sets of field values and use them in our charts instead of the current selection. In our first KPI dashboard, we need to show groupings of accounts based on the **Acct_Group** or **Nature** data columns to get the correct calculations.

> Set expressions are only available for charts and not in scripts.

Set expressions always begin and end with curly brackets. For example, sum({1} Amount), where {1} is a set expression represented using the shortcut expression {1}.

Building our set expressions

Under normal circumstances, you could build one chart with the dimension **Nature** and the measure **sum (Amount)**. User selections of **Company** and **AcctGroup** would then determine what is shown. However, here, we want our chart or gauge to always show the same ratio and to only be affected by date selections and individual company selections. An initial, but longwinded, set expression for ROA for our sample data would look like the following, but, as we continue, we will learn how to shorten these statements into set expressions that QlikView will understand:

```
set_expression= { all of Amount< for Nature IS >}/{all of Amount < for
Nature Assets>}
set_expression= { current selection of Amount< for Nature IS >}/
{current selection of Amount < for Nature Assets>}
```

Here, Nature IS and Nature Assets are values originally from a column of information named Nature that we loaded to QlikView.

To state an initial set expression for ROI for our sample dataset, the set expression would look similar to this:

```
set_expression= { all of Amount< for Nature IS >}/({all of Amount <
for Nature LT_Liabilities >} + {all of Amount < for Nature Equity >})
set_expression= { current selection of Amount< for Nature IS >}/
({current selection of Amount < for Nature LT_Liabilities>} + {current
selection of Amount < for Nature Equity>})
```

To state an initial set expression for ROE for our sample dataset, the set expression would be similar to this:

```
set_expression= { all of Amount< for Nature IS >}/{all of Amount < for
Nature Equity >}
set_expression= { current selection of Amount< for Nature IS >} /
{current selection of Amount < for Nature Equity>}
```

But we can make our expression simpler using expression shortcuts. Expression shortcuts that we can use are as follows:

- The qualifier for `all` is `1`.
- The qualifier for current selection is `$`

And the syntax for modifiers in this case is as follows:

```
set_modifier = <field_name={field_value,[field_value]}
```

Using the shortcuts, we get the KPI measures for our charts, which use set expressions:

```
=sum({1<Nature={IS}>} Amount) / sum({1<Nature={Assets}>} Amount)
=sum({$<Nature={IS}>} Amount)/ sum({$<Nature={Assets}>} Amount)
```

Our **Sales** are credits and our **Assets** are credits (negative numbers) as they come from the ledger source system in order for our trial balance in the previous chapter to work. We need to make one more change to our formula to compensate for our net income being negative when it is more than our expenses. We multiply each formula line by minus one. So, here's how our expression now looks:

```
=(sum({1<Nature={IS}>} Amount) / sum({1<Nature={Assets}>} Amount)) *
(-1)
=(sum({$<Nature={IS}>} Amount)/ sum({$<Nature={Assets}>} Amount)) *
(-1)
```

Expression shortcuts

Expression shortcuts known as *Set Identifiers* define the relationship between the set expression and field values (columns) or the expression that is being evaluated. Set identifiers can be combined using set operators, which follow the rules of mathematical operators.

In addition to the two expression shortcuts that we used earlier, there are a few other shortcuts that we might want to use. The following are navigational expressions that allow us to use previous calculations for forward calculations, comparisons, and trending-type operations:

- $N where N is a number representing the previous evaluation expression to use. For example, $1 means use the previous selections, and $0 means use the current selections.

- $_N where N is a number representing the number of forward steps in an evaluation. For example, $_1 means the next step in the selections.

These only work if you have made backward and forward navigational steps within a QlikView sheet object. Once you have made selections and changed them, the **Back** button and the **Forward** button become available to flip back and forth through the prior selection:

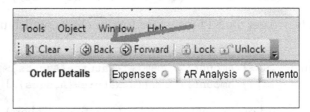

Figure 2-4: Here, the Back and Forward buttons are enabled

Mathematical and set operators

There are several set operators that look similar to what we think of as mathematical operators that can be used in set expressions. Their meaning and function is determined by where they are used in the set expression. All the set operators use sets as the operands and return a set as the result. Within a group, the set expression is evaluated from left to right just as a mathematical expression would be evaluated. So, it is necessary to group expressions using standard parentheses () to indicate how an expression should be evaluated. For example, X + (Y - Z) is not the same as (X + Y) - Z and is also different than (X-Z) + Y where X, Y and Z are sets rather than individual numbers. This makes it even more important to designate the evaluation order with parentheses in set expressions because we are actually working with groups of numbers instead of simple math.

According to the help feature of QlikView, we should avoid using fields from multiple QlikView tables, as we did in making our **Sales** versus **Target** ratio in set expressions, because the results can be unpredictable.

For example, sum({1-$<AcctGroup={Sales}>}) returns the sales for everything excluded by the current selection because of the *Exclusion Set Operator* between the 1 and the $.

Operators	Name of Operator and its functionality
+	**Union**. This operator returns a set of the records that belong to <u>any</u> of the two set operands.
-	**Exclusion**. This operator returns a set of the records that belong to the first but not the other of the two set operands. It can also be used to return the complement of a single set. For example sum({1-$} Amount) returns our Amount totaled for everything not currently selected.
*	**Intersection**. This operator returns a set consisting of the records that belong to both of the two set operands.
/	**Symmetric difference (XOR)**. This operator returns a set consisting of the records that belong to either, but not both of the two set operands.

Creating our three-KPI display

Now, we will add the ROA-, ROI-, and ROE-type gauges to the KPIs tab. Prepare by copying our **Sales** tab and pasting it as a new sheet. Rename the sheet KPIs. You can delete your **Sales** vs **Target** object if you want, or experiment with minimizing it.

Next, we will make our three returns KPIs. Choose **Charts**, and **Chart Wizard** will pop up. These are the steps to making the thermometer-type gauge that we want to display for each measure:

1. On the **General** tab, title your object Return on Assets, and select the **Gauge Chart** type by clicking on the button.

2. Now, click on **NEXT**.

3. On the **Dimensions** tab, select **Nature**, **Amount**, and **Month** in the **Used Dimension** box.

4. Click on **NEXT**.

5. On the **Expressions** tab, enter this formula in **Expression Box** as it appears here:

   ```
   =(sum({$<Nature={IS}>} Amount) / sum({$<Nature={Assets}>} Amount))
   * (-1)
   ```

6. Click on **OK**, and then click on **Add** to add another expression. Enter this expression:

   ```
   =(sum({1<Nature={IS}>} Amount)/ sum({1<Nature={Assets}>} Amount))
   * (-1)
   ```

   Having the two expressions enables us to use the **Back** button in QlikView.

7. Make sure that your expressions show up in **Expression Box**.

8. Click on **Next**.

9. Leave the **Sort** tab as it is and click on **Next**.

10. On the **Style** tab, select the blue test tube-type indicator:

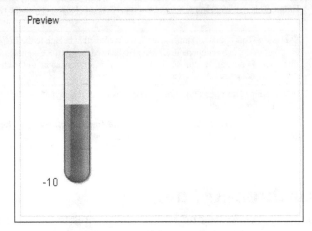

Figure 2-5: Preview of the test tube-type gauge

11. In the **Presentation** tab, change **Min** to **-10** and **Max** to **10**.

12. Click on **Finish**.

Repeat the preceding steps for `Return on Investment` using these two formulas:

```
=(sum({$<Nature={IS}>} Amount) / (sum({$<Nature={Equity}>} Amount) +
sum({$<Nature={LT_Liabilities}>} Amount)) )
=(sum({1<Nature={IS}>} Amount) / (sum({1<Nature={Equity}>} Amount) +
sum({1<Nature={LT_Liabilities}>} Amount)) )
```

Size your boxes with the KPIs to approximately the same size, and then repeat the steps for Return on Equity using these two formulas:

```
=(sum({$<Nature={IS}>} Amount) / (sum({$<Nature={Equity}>} Amount)) )
* (-1)
=(sum({1<Nature={IS}>} Amount) / (sum({1<Nature={Equity}>} Amount)) )
* (-1)
```

Size your boxes with the KPIs to approximately the same size and arrange them in order on the sheet. Your KPIs tab should look somewhat similar to the next screenshot:

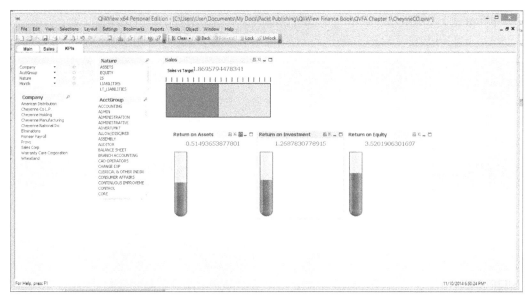

Figure 2-6: The KPIs tab with completed KPI gauges

Use the **Multi Box** or **List Box** to change your KPIs and watch the numbers and levels change.

What happens if you reverse the set operation formulas by reversing their order and promoting one over the other so that the one using $ is first?

```
=(sum({$<Nature={IS}>} Amount)/ sum({$<Nature={Assets}>} Amount)) *
(-1)
=(sum({1<Nature={IS}>} Amount) / sum({1<Nature={Assets}>} Amount)) *
(-1)
```

The **KPIs** are frozen at the All-level selection because we have moved that expression to the top of the two expressions for each KPI display.

For additional information, see the help feature of QlikView. You can also examine the various QlikView applications that can be downloaded when you install QlikView. You will find them in the `Install` folder. `Data Visualization`, in particular, has examples of all the chart display types. We will investigate more of these in the following chapters.

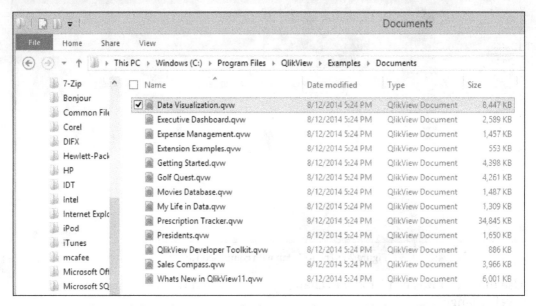

Figure 2-7: Examples to examine the documents that came with the installation

Common size income statement

My favorite KPI to implement in a dashboard is an extension of the **Return on Sales** ratio. This KPI or set of ratios is formally called *Common size income statement* but is often seen in an income statement as a percentage of **Sales**. I first came across this in an international business class on evaluating company profitability through financial statement analysis.

 There is an additional sample data Excel spreadsheet available for download from your account at `http://www.PacktPub.com` that is used in this chapter. Its name is `IS3yr.xls`.

Common size income statement lends itself particularly well to dashboards presented as a period-over-period line graph that allows you to see the shape and trend of the data, rather than just the numbers.

To create a common size income statement, start with the key subtotals of a standard income statement divided by total revenue. Here is an example of **XYZ Company** from an income statement template with a percentage of **Sales** column:

Income Statement

XYZ Company, Inc.
For Period Ending June 30, 2009
(all numbers in $000)

	2007		2008		2009	
	Amount	% of Sales	Amount	% of Sales	Amount	% of Sales
REVENUE						
Gross Sales	$2,525		$2,693		$2,941	
Less sales returns and allowances	450		500		510	
Net Sales	$2,075	100%	$2,193	100%	$2,431	100%
COST OF SALES						
Beginning inventory	$350	17%	$360	16%	$370	17%
Plus goods purchased / manufactured	850	41%	900	41%	925	42%
Total Goods Available	$1,200	58%	$1,260	57%	$1,295	59%
Less ending inventory	360	17%	370	17%	360	16%
Total Cost of Goods Sold	$840	40%	$890	41%	$935	43%
Gross Profit (Loss)	$1,235	65%	$1,303	59%	$1,496	68%
OPERATING EXPENSES						
Selling						
Salaries and wages	$125	6%	$130	6%	$135	6%
Commissions	82	4%	84	4%	86	4%
Advertising	50	12%	60	3%	65	3%
Depreciation	120	6%	120	5%	120	5%
Other	30	1%	33	1%	34	2%
Total Selling Expenses	$407	28%	$428	20%	$440	20%
General/Administrative						
Salaries and wages	$126	6%	$129	6%	$131	6%
Employee benefits	31	1%	33	2%	34	2%
Payroll taxes	23	1%	24	1%	25	1%
Insurance	2	0%	2	0%	2	0%
Rent	23	1%	23	1%	23	1%
Utilities	30	1%	32	1%	34	2%
Depreciation & amortization	18	1%	16	1%	16	1%
Office supplies	9	0%	8	0%	8	0%
Travel & entertainment	4	0%	5	0%	4	0%
Postage	11	1%	12	1%	12	1%
Equipment maintenance & rental	49	2%	49	2%	49	2%
Interest	31	1%	31	1%	30	1%
Furniture & equipment	12	1%	11	1%	9	0%
Total General/Administrative Expenses	$369	18%	$375	17%	$377	17%
Total Operating Expenses	$776	37%	$804	37%	$817	37%
Net Income Before Taxes	$459	22%	$499	23%	$679	31%
Taxes on income	137	7%	151	7%	174	8%
Net Income After Taxes	$322	15%	$348	16%	$505	23%
Extraordinary gain or loss	$0	0%	$0	0%	$0	0%
Income tax on extraordinary gain	0	0%	0	0%	0	0%
NET INCOME (LOSS)	$322	15%	$348	16%	$505	23%

Figure 2-8: XYZ Company's income statement year-over-year with percentage of Sales

This is a very useful document, particularly if we have drilldown capabilities, but it definitely requires time to review the comparisons. If we look at the bottom line, we can see that **Net Income** has not only gone up, but has gone up as a percent of **Sales**. But this is not the information that we want a dashboard to convey quickly. This is what we would use with the drilldown to investigate the underlying details. Now, we want to bring those percentiles into a month/year-over-month/year line graph.

We begin by loading our year-over-year spreadsheet to a QlikView document.

1. Choose **Edit Script** from the **File** menu.
2. Place your cursor below any other scripting.
3. Click on **Table** Files.
4. Navigate to IS3yr.xlsx, your downloaded spreadsheet.
5. Select your spreadsheet to load, and then switch **Labels** to embedded.
6. Click on **Finish**.

Your script should look like this, except for the path of IS3yr.xls:

```
LOAD NewCompany,
    Group,
    Account,
    [2007],
    [2008],
    [2009],
    [2007 ROS],
    [2008 ROS],
    [2009 ROS]
FROM
[C:\Users\User\Documents\My Docs\Packt Publishing\QlikView Finance
Book\QVFA Chapter2\IS3yr.xls]
(ooxml, embedded labels, table is IS3yr);
```

 Notice that if you are still using the same QlikView document, the column label is **NewCompany** so that QlikView doesn't try to join **XYZ Company** with **Cheyenne Manufacturing**.

Now, we will create our line graph for a common size income statement.

Create a new **Sheet** tab if desired:

1. Right-click on the background of the current sheet to bring up the context menu and choose **New Sheet Object**.

2. Then, choose **Chart**.

3. On the **General** tab, give our chart the title Common Size Income Statement.

4. Check the box to use **Show Title** in the **Chart** and enter XYZ Company Inc.

5. Choose the **Line Graph-type** chart (**#2** of the chart types in *Figure 1* of this chapter):

6. On the **Dimensions** tab, choose **Account**.

7. On the **Expressions** tab, add three expressions by choosing the **Value Only** aggregation type and each of the three ROS measures in turn so that the three expressions look similar to this:

```
Only ([2007 ROS])
Only ([2008 ROS])
Only ([2009 ROS])
```

8. Now, use **Label** on each expression so that the legend will display 2007, 2008, and 2009.

9. In the **Sort** tab, choose the checkbox for **Load Order** and clear the other checkboxes.

10. On the **Numbers** tab, switch from **Default** to **Number** and check the **Show in Percent** checkbox.

11. Click on **Finish** and adjust the size of the QlikView screen and **Chart Object** to get the best visual presentation. The ONLY in the expression used previously is an aggregation expression that acts as a group to return one aggregated number from the group or NULL if there isn't a match to the selections.

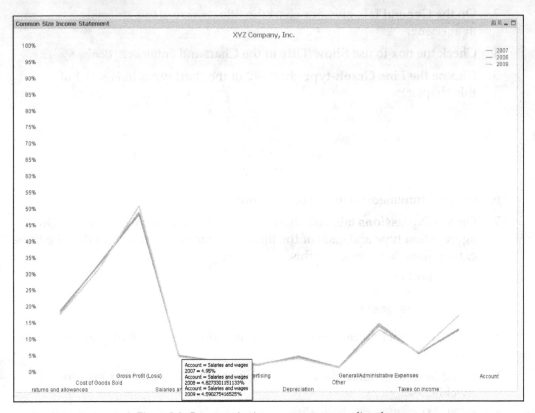

Figure 2-9: Common size income statement as a line chart

Navigate around our new chart. Notice that you can get popup boxes with the information that gives the exact percentages for the area. You can select a year from the **Legend** and highlight the entire line by thickening it. If you click on a point, the graph will change to a percent range showing each of the 3 years as dots.

You can hover over the dots to get the information; the distance between the dots is increased so that they are easier to compare. Use the **Clear** button to return to **Chart** and show the original display.

In our new chart, we can make the following observations:

In this line graph, we can see that, overall, we have managed quite well in June 2009. Our net profit has increased in comparison to our costs and expenses, but we already knew that from our income statement.

We can see that this is, in part, because we have controlled our advertising expenses compared to 2007 without hurting our sales.

We can also see that we have kept our taxes in the same bracket with only slight increases.

Our total G&A expenses have gone up disproportionately to the preceding year, so we would want to examine that in more detail to see whether there are potential cost savings or if, perhaps, we have created new jobs giving us tax breaks, thereby increasing our net profit margin.

Because the lines are so close together (we are using the numbers from the sample Income Statement shown earlier in this chapter), we might want to change our image to a bar chart. To do this, right-click on **Common Size Income Statement**, which we have been examining, and on the **General** tab under the **Chart Type** section, choose the **Bar Chart** (**#1** in *Figure 1* of this chapter). Now, our chart looks similar to the next image:

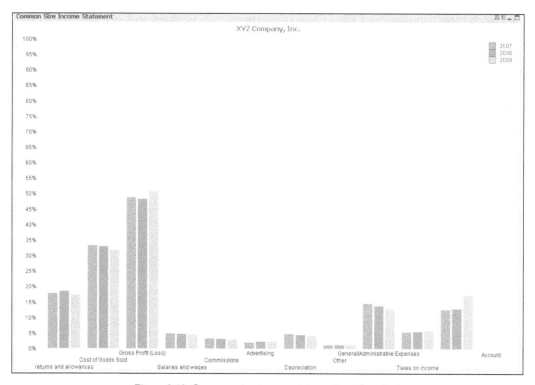

Figure 2-10: Common size income statement as a bar chart

We also want to keep in mind the timing variances that might affect a particular month. Because of the potential for timing variances, we would want to be able to look at total year-over-total year at the year's end to forecast for the coming year. We will examine a year-over-year-by-month combination bar and a line chart in *Chapter 5, QlikView Sales Analysis*.

Other things that are readily visible are that we have kept our cost of goods sold in line, whilst increasing our gross profit margin, and kept the growth in salaries and wages to produce sales in parallel with the growth in sales. This might possibly indicate that increasing our sales force would increase our profits further.

We instantly get a day-to-day visual of how we are managing our sales and expenses compared to prior years, and, when the month closes, how we have done.

No KPI or dashboard widget will replace experience and business common sense, but good dashboard KPIs can lead an executive to ask the questions that will lead to business improvement.

Summary

In this chapter, you learned about key performance indicators and several different ways of creating visual displays of them in QlikView. We began creating set expressions and used expression shortcuts. We created three KPI gauges for Return on Investment, Return on Assets, and Return on Expenses. We created a common size income statement chart and did some analysis of that chart to see how visualization can be useful in data comparison.

In the next chapter, we will begin examining a QlikView example dashboard for a chief financial officer, where we will examine more KPIs and more QlikView objects to see how they are used in this dashboard.

3
KPIs in the Financial Officer QlikView Dashboard

In the previous chapter, we built our first KPI display. Now, we will use one of the examples we downloaded when we installed QlikView to learn about other ways to display KPIs that might interest a **Chief Financial Officer** (CFO).

In this chapter, we will cover the following topics:

- An example QlikView CFO dashboard — the KPIs tab
- The good, the bad, and the ugly — the display for the KPIs tab
- The nuts and bolts of the KPIs tab:
    - Sheet objects
    - The script

Opening the example CFO dashboard

1. Open QlikView if it is not open already.
2. Using the **File | Open** menu in QlikView, navigate to the **Program Files | QlikView | Examples | Documents** folder and double-click on Executive Dashboard.qvw to open.
3. After reading the information on the first tab that explains that this is the CFO dashboard, select the second tab — that is, the KPIs tab.

4. The screen will look similar to the following screenshot:

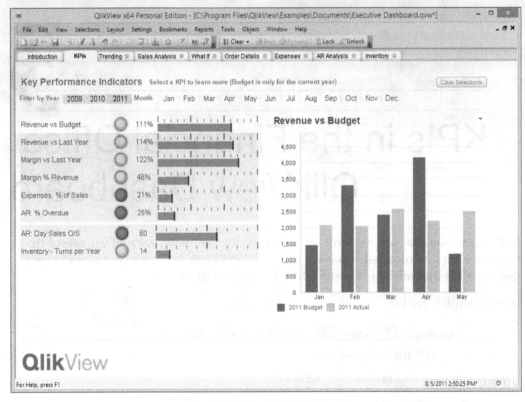

Figure 3-1: KPIs on CFO dashboard

Notice the other tabs:

- **Trending**
- **Sales Analysis**
- **What If**
- **Order Details**
- **Expenses**
- **AR Analysis**
- **Inventory**

This would seem to cover nearly everything needed by a CFO to manage the business.

In this chapter and the following chapters, we are going to examine each of the tabs, and I will point out the good and bad features from a design standpoint. Then, we will look at how to produce similar displays.

The KPIs tab in a nutshell

The **KPIs** tab has very good display choices. The months and years are readily visible, inviting selections. The use of the red/green stoplight combined with the slider bar actually functions as a selection box to change the bar graph. So, when selecting a specific KPI, we immediately see whether or not the measure is above or below budget. If our CFO happens to be red/green color-blind, we might want to switch our stoplight colors to blue and yellow or other alternating pictures (although happy faces and frowning faces are probably considered juvenile). The budget data is only loaded for 2011 for demonstration purposes.

 Don't forget that, sometimes, numbers will need to be reversed in order to be displayed in the correct way, such as when we multiplied **Sales** by **-1** in the previous chapter.

Click on **Expenses: % of Sales**, and you will notice that the bar chart adds a red line graph to represent the current year's (2011) budget. Other than that special case, the bar chart either just displays the KPI by month or displays the KPI and the budgeted KPI.

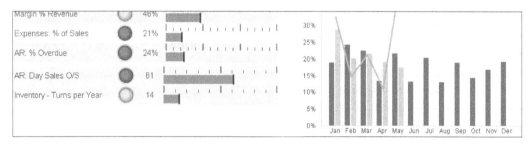

Figure 3-2: KPIs on the CFO dashboard

Delving into sheet objects

Across the top of sheet, we have three text objects. The first one is formatted to show the title of the page: **Key Performance Indicators**. By right-clicking on the first text object, we can choose **Properties** and examine the properties that can be set for the text object. Each **Text Object Properties** wizard has five tabs:

- **General**
- **Actions**
- **Font**
- **Layout**
- **Caption**

In the case of the text object title, the only properties that are set are on the **General** tab and the **Font** tab. The **General** tab contains the foreground text to display and the background color. The **Font** tab has the font display choices. We would use the **Layout** tab to create borders around the text object, if desired.

The second text object contains instructions and, like the title, just uses the **General** tab and the **Font** tab.

The third text object in the first row

The third text object in the first row of objects is a little more interesting. It looks like a button and, indeed, if clicked on, it has an action—to clear all the selections. Look at the **Properties** of the text object that looks like a button that says **Clear All**. On the very first tab, the **General** tab, we can see that it is indeed a picture instead of text such as the title. This particular picture even has the words **Clear All** right in it. We just learned that text objects can actually contain pictures. An actual **Button** object could have been used instead of the text object with **Actions**. Either object functions the same way based on the **Actions** associated with it.

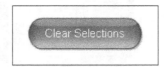

Figure 3-3: The Button object created to clear selections

Several kinds of picture formats can be used: bitmaps (`.bmp`), jpegs (`.jpg` or `.jpeg`), graphic interchange formats (`.gif`), and portable network graphics (`.png`) will be the types listed if you click on the radio button for **Image** and then the **Change...** button to choose an image.

On the **Actions** tab, there is a box that shows what **Action** is selected, if any. This particular instance of text object has the **Clear All** action selected. If you click on the **Add** button below the box, then the types of actions are displayed on the left-hand side. And when you select one of the action types, the different actions associated with that **Action** type are displayed on the right-hand side to be selected.

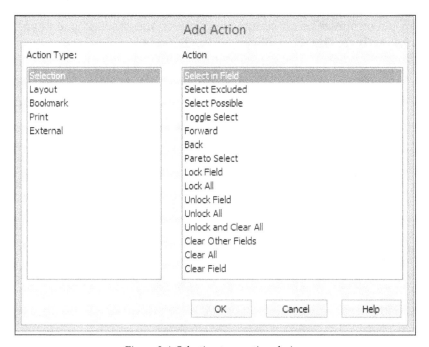

Figure 3-4: Selection type action choices

There are five action types for text objects:

1. **Selection**: These actions can be linked to what happens in our other sheet objects being displayed. This is where the **Clear All** action comes from. We can create other actions that occur *on click*, such as **Select Excluded**, **Toggle Select**, **Lock Field**, **Unlock**, and **Clear All**. **Selection** has the most menu items in its wizard. QlikView help lists all of the selections and what they do.

One **Selection** action that probably needs further explanation is **Pareto Select**. To make a pareto selection in the specified field, it should be based on an expression and a percentage. This type of selection is used to select the top contributors to a measure, typically defaulting to a general 80/20 rule. For example, to find the top sales outlet that contributes to 80 percent of the sales, **Sales Outlet** should be used as the field, **sum (Sales)** should be used as the expression, and **80** should be used as the percentage.

In any wizard dialog with the ellipses (...) button, it is possible to enter a calculated formula.

2. **Layout**: The second **Action type**, **Layout**, works to move between sheets, such as web page links, or to change the size of sheet objects. For example, you can minimize or maximize the graph on the sheet. Related to webpage links, **Activate Object** also works in web mode.

To switch to web mode, navigate to the **View** menu at the top of the QlikView interface and then scroll down the **View** menu popup to choose the **Turn on/off** WebView toggle. For now, we will work with WebView off. Working with WebView to create objects requires drag-and-drop techniques, and they will not be covered in this book. If you are interested in learning more about objects in WebView, please see my previous book about QlikView: *Instant QlikView Application Development*, also published by Packt Publishing.

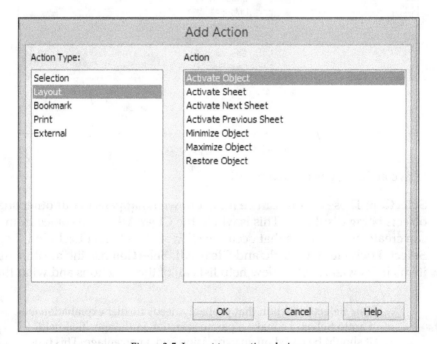

Figure 3-5: Layout type action choices

3. **Bookmark**: **Bookmark** actions are the third **Action type**. They also work like web page links by allowing us to create actions that move the QlikView user from one page tab to another page tab. You can see this in action by going back to the CFO dashboard **Introduction** tab and clicking on the deep-blue colored **Get Started** button. The button then takes you to the **KPIs** tab that we are currently examining.

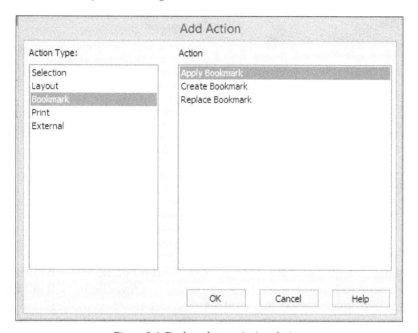

Figure 3-6: Bookmark type Action choices

 Bookmarks can also be created independent of **Text Box** actions with other Sheet objects using the **Bookmark** menu at the top of the QlikView document. Here, you can add, replace, or remove **Bookmark**. **More…** in the **Bookmark** menu allows you to view all the Bookmarks in a QlikView document.

4. **Print**: **Print** actions are the fourth set of actions available. From **Print** actions, you can choose **Print Object**, **Print Sheet**, and **Print Report**. How well these actions work depends on how much QlikView is allowed to interact with your computer environment. **Print Report** specifically needs **Reports** designed to interact with it. **Reports** can be designed through the QlikView Reports menu at the top of a QlikView document; this has one option, **Edit Reports**. Learning to design QlikView **Print Reports** is beyond the scope of this book.

5. **External**: The final set of actions available is **External**.

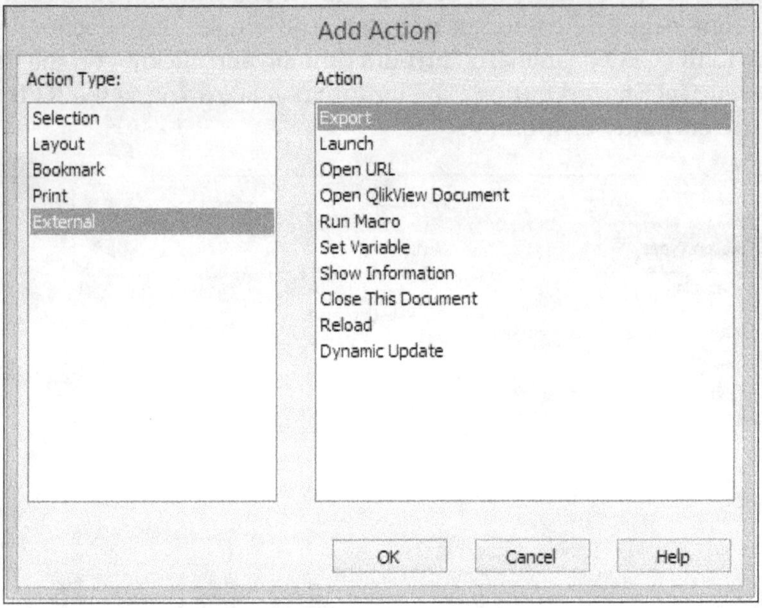

Figure 3-7: External type Action choices

The use of **External** actions is highly dependent on how much QlikView is allowed to interact with the environment. A few clients will not handle these settings and most **External** actions only function in WebView or when connected to QlikView server. Some run only with the proprietary *QlikView Server Ajax ZFC* client, and others will not run with the Ajax client. If your QlikView application for your CFO or other C level officer is going to need one of these specific functionalities, please review the requirements in QlikView help, and coordinate with your technology department for application and environment support.

The actions available from the **External** actions menu are explained next:

- **Export**: This exports a table containing a specific set of fields, but only those records that are applicable according to the sheet selection are exported.

- **Launch**: This launches an external program, such as Excel or Word.

  It has parameters to be specified, such as:

  - **Application** : This is the program that should be launched

  - **Filename**: The path to the file that should be opened with the application specified earlier

○ **Parameters**: This includes any additional information needed for the program being launched

○ **Working Directory**: This sets the directory for the application to be launched

○ **Exit application**: This forces the application to be closed when QlikView is closed

 Launch will not function as a document and sheet trigger.

○ **Open URL** opens the URL specified in the default web browser.

○ **Open QlikView Document** opens the specified QlikView document:

○ The file extension must be included.

○ Mark the **Transfer State** checkbox to transfer the selections from the original document to the one you wish to open. The opened document will first be cleared of selections. Mark **Apply State** on top of the current to retain the second document's selections and apply the original document's selections on top of them.

 Using **Apply State** on top of the current document can cause unpredictable results if the two document selections are conflicting. Using the **Transfer State** option should be sufficient in most cases.

○ **Open in same window** opens the new document in the same browser tab but only when using a QlikView server environment with the AJAX ZFC client.

 The **Open QlikView document** action is not supported when using the Internet Explorer plugin. This does not mean that it will not work, depending upon the version of Internet Explorer. It is only that it is not supported (not guaranteed to work).

○ **Run Macro** allows the running of an external macro:

○ Enter the path and name of the macro to be run.

○ Type a name for the macro that you have already created or will create later in the **Edit Module** dialog. You can also do this in a calculated expression for dynamic updates.

- ° **Set Variable** assigns a value to the specified variable.

- ° **Show Information** shows the associated information, such as a text file or an image for the field specified by **Field**. This function does not work in the AJAX ZFC client.

- ° **Close This Document** closes the active QlikView document.

- ° **Reload** performs a reload on the current document. This function does not work in the AJAX ZFC client.

- ° **Dynamic Update** performs a dynamic update of the data in the currently loaded document. The intended usage of **Dynamic Update** allows a QlikView administrator to feed limited amounts of data into a QlikView document from a single source without running a reload of the document. Analysis can then be performed by multiple clients connecting to QlikView server.

 The uploaded information is only stored in RAM. Any data added or updated using **Dynamic Update** will be lost if the document is reloaded.

The second row of sheet objects

In the second row of sheet objects, we find alternating text objects to describe the list boxes. So, the words **Filter by Year** are in a text object, and the actual years that can be selected are in a **List Box** displayed as **2009 | 2010 | 2011** and available for selection. Next comes another text object that identifies that the next **List Box** contains **Month** for selection. What we have failed to notice is that there is actually a sheet object between the first row of text and the second row of text. If you right-click the pale-blue line in between and choose **Properties**, you will see that it is a **Line/Arrow object []** with three linked objects. Using **Properties** in the **General** tab, experiment with making Line/Arrow objects appear in different colors.

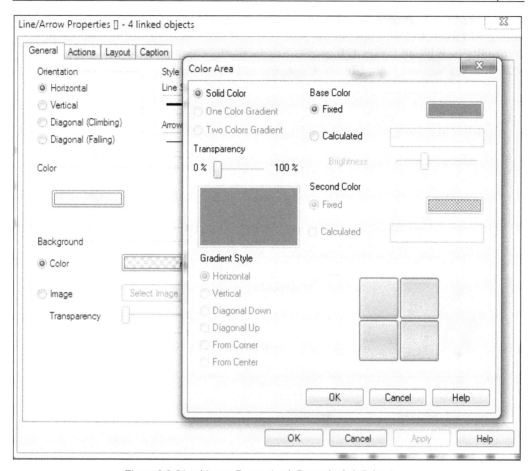

Figure 3-8: Line/Arrow Properties | General tab | Color Area

The third row of sheet objects

What looks like a third row of sheet objects is actually an interconnected set of text objects with **Actions** and layered charts, along with a block of layered, invisible charts made visible by **Set Variable Action**. So, when we click on a row with the stoplight circle, we are actually selecting a text object and that, in turn, makes the associated blue bar chart visible. The first stoplight row, **Revenue vs Budget** , is text object TX103 and passes the **vShowChart** variable set to a value of **1**. This makes chart object CH54 visible because, in the **Layout** tab of the **Properties** chart, the **Show section** picks up the **vShowChart** variable when the value is **1**. The next stoplight row in the table-like structure uses the same variable **vShowChart** (as does each of the other rows), but the variable is set to equal 2 (or 3, 4, and so on) to control its associated chart.

The **Layout** tab of **Properties** also contains the **Layer** designation. There are three standard **Layer** designations — **Top**, **Normal**, and **Bottom** — corresponding to the internally numbered layers **1**, **0**, and **-1**, respectively. Custom layer values between **-128** and **127** are accepted. Choose **Custom** to enter a value of your choice.

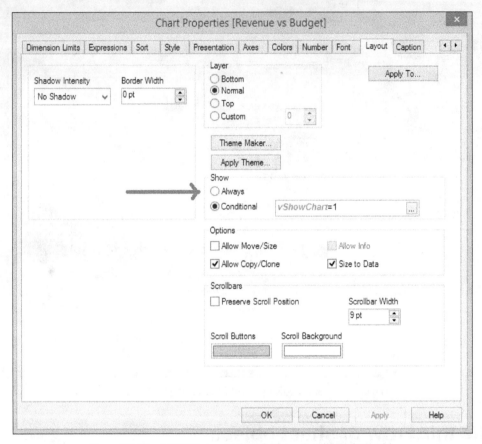

Figure 3-9: Chart CH54 Layout tab with Show Conditional Variable

An additional chart object is layered under the rows of Text objects. For each row of the table-like structure, they use images to display the appropriate red or green circle images as an **Image Chart** object. **Next in Chart** object, **Text Chart** object is used to display the percentage. Finally, to get the bar line, **Linear Gauge** is used. These are all a single chart object with multiple displays. For example, for the last text object row in the KPIs measures block — **Inventory-Turns per Year** — the three charts in the chart object are set up in the following manner:

On the **Dimension Limits** tab, the dimension used is this formula:

```
=If([Dashboard Metric]='AR: Day Sales O/S' or [Dashboard
Metric]='Inventory - Turns p77781er Year',[Dashboard Metric])
```

Then, on the **Expressions** tab, we have three representations of the same information. The first is **Image**, the second **Text**, and the third **Linear Gauge**:

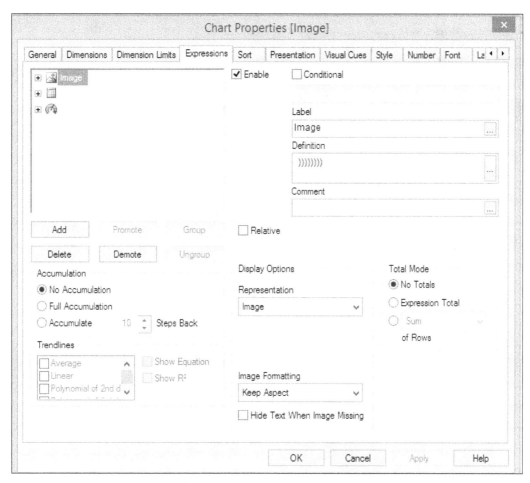

Figure 3-10: The Expressions tab with three chart types selected

Only the stoplight image chart has a definition entered on the **Expressions** tab. In the previous image, we can see the tail end of the expression definition with eight parentheses. The definition is an expression that tells the chart to flip between the red and green images. This is the definition code used for the *Inventory – Turns per Year*:

```
If([Dashboard Metric]='Inventory - Turns per Year',
    If((Sum(ThroughputQty*CostPrice)/Sum(StockOH*CostPrice))>10,'qmem:/
/<bundled>/BuiltIn/led_g.png',
    If((Sum(ThroughputQty*CostPrice)/Sum(StockOH*CostPrice))<=10 and
(Sum(ThroughputQty*CostPrice)/Sum(StockOH*CostPrice))>5,'qmem://<bundl
ed>/BuiltIn/led_g.png',
```

```
     If((Sum(ThroughputQty*CostPrice)/Sum(StockOH*CostPrice))<=5,'qmem:/
/<bundled>/BuiltIn/led_g.png')))
)))))))))
```

The parts of the code line in single quotes with the extension .png are the image files and their paths. We will create our own image display in *Chapter 9, QlikView Expenses Dashboard.*

Load script for the KPIs dashboard tab

The following is the load script used with the KPIs dashboard tab. It has the standard English language settings for date and time formats and thousands separator. If we had chosen a different language, other standard settings would be part of the script. The very first line with the word Binary is loading data and dimensions from another QlikView document. It must come first in the script and loads very fast. As you read more of the script, you can also notice that, for function commands such as SET, LET, and NUM, the script is case-insensitive:

```
Binary [executive dashboard.qvw];

SET ThousandSep=',';
SET DecimalSep='.';
SET MoneyThousandSep=',';
SET MoneyDecimalSep='.';
SET MoneyFormat='$#,##0.00;($#,##0.00)';
SET TimeFormat='h:mm:ss TT';
SET DateFormat='M/D/YYYY';
SET TimestampFormat='M/D/YYYY h:mm:ss[.fff] TT';
SET MonthNames='Jan;Feb;Mar;Apr;May;Jun;Jul;Aug;Sep;Oct;Nov;Dec';
SET DayNames='Mon;Tue;Wed;Thu;Fri;Sat;Sun';

LET vCurrentMonthNum = NUM(Month(Makedate(Year(Today()),5,31)));
LET vCurrentMonth = Month(Makedate(Year(Today()),5,31));
Let vCurrentYear = num(year(today()));
Let vTodaysDate = num(today());
Let v12month = num(Makedate(Year(Today())-1,5,31));
Let vRolling12months = Num#($(v12month),'YYYYMM');
LET vOldDate = num(Makedate(2003,5,31));
LET vTodaysDate = num(Makedate(Year(Today()),5,31));
LET vToday = (Makedate(Year(Today()),5,31));
LET vAdjDays = $(vTodaysDate) - $(vOldDate); //the gap between july
2003 and today
```

```
LOAD * INLINE [
  Display as
  Dollars
  Percentage
];

[Dasboard Metrics]:
LOAD * INLINE [
  Dashboard Metric
  Revenue vs Budget
  Revenue vs Last Year
  Margin vs Last Year
  Margin % Revenue
  Expenses: % of Sales
  AR: % Overdue
  AR: Day Sales O/S
  Inventory - Turns per Year
];
```

After the language-related standards are defined with SET statements, we use LET statements to define global variables, such as the current date, current month, and current year. SET statements assign a specific value to a variable. LET statements use expressions to calculate based on the values assigned to the variables within the expression. That is why LET statements should come before SET statements in your script.

Following the LET statements, we can see that the data is loaded INLINE. This means that we will type the data into the script and not load it from an Excel or other file. We use the **Inline Data Wizard** for help with the creation of LOAD INLINE statements.

The **Inline Data Wizard** dialog is opened from the menu path:

File | Edit Script | Insert menu | Load Statement | Load Inline

This wizard is used to create the load inline statements in the script. The following screenshot shows this:

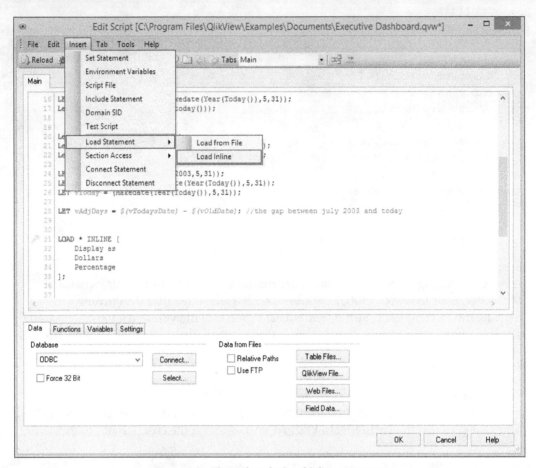

Figure 3-11: The path to the Load Inline statement

The wizard contains something that looks similar to a spreadsheet and, in fact, works much like one. However, calculation formulas will not be evaluated in this spreadsheet as they would in Excel.

Each column represents a field to be loaded into QlikView in a manner similar to the Excel spreadsheets we used in *Chapter 1, Getting That Financial Data into QlikView* and *Chapter 2, QlikView Dashboard Financial KPIs*. Just as with the Excel spreadsheets we used, each row is a record in the table. A data cell is selected by clicking on it. A value can then be typed or pasted from the clipboard. Just as with Excel, press *Enter* or any arrow key to accept the value and move to another cell.

The top (label) row of the inline wizard data entry form is reserved for the dimension labels. Double-click in a label cell to enter a name. If no custom labels are entered in the label row, the field names F1, F2, and so on will be used.

Summary

In this chapter, we examined the KPIs tab of the example CFO dashboard in detail. You now know what objects were used on sheet and how they are layered to create a specific design look. You learned how to set up **Actions** within a text object or button. You now know how to use variables to make a chart visible or not visible. We looked at **Line/Arrow Object Properties** and changed the line color. We saw that it is possible to use text objects to contain variables that control chart objects. We examined the script and learned about Binary loads of other QlikView documents. We learned that chart objects can contain more than one chart controlled by variables. And we now know that data can be entered inline to produce specific display results.

In the next chapter, you will learn more about options when it comes to loading data into QlikView from multiple sources.

4
QlikView Asset Management with Multiple Data Sources

Whether we are discussing capital assets (such as property, plant and equipment) or production assets (such as inventory) or financial instrument assets (such as stocks, bonds, and partnership investment), an important part of any financial operation is asset management. Often, we think of private banking and wealth management businesses with respect to financial instrument assets. The datasets can be very large, and data from many different sources needs to be combined to get the big picture. This process is often manual in many organizations where Excel is used to perform analysis, usually with poor and often untimely results.

A powerful business intelligence platform can be leveraged for wealth management, asset management, and private banking institutions to increase analysis productivity greatly. Therefore, this chapter will look at an example of financial instrument asset management with a QlikView dashboard other than CFO Dashboard, which we have been examining. Then, we will examine the loading scripts of multiple data sources as they might be used to load an asset management QlikView document.

We will return to tabs within CFO Dashboard to examine *Inventory and Forecasting* in later chapters.

Assets under management (financial investments)

Open the **QlikView Asset Management** example dashboard located at

```
http://eu-a.demo.qlik.com/QvAJAXZfc/opendoc.
htm?document=qvdocs%2FAsset%20Management.
qvw&host=demo11&anonymous=true
```

The first tab, **Intro**, of the **QlikView Asset Management** dashboard will look similar to the following screenshot:

Figure 4-1: Asset Management dashboard

As we can see in the first tab, the most important thing about an **Assets Under Management** (financial investment assets) dashboard is obtaining data from multiple sources. In this dashboard, we have the data that we entered, such as the Excel spreadsheets we uploaded or data that we input inline. Additionally, we have data from web sources, such as **Imagine**, **Bloomberg**, **Advent**, **Factset**, **RiskMetricsGroup**, and **Princeton**. Notice that the green lines with dots document the source attribution, with the different sections of the picture of the dashboard located on the next tab, the **Dashboard** tab.

This is a server-based QlikView dashboard, so it is locked down. We cannot see the scripts or the actual sources used to feed this dashboard. This is why, as we continue, we will use example scripts to introduce many of the data-loading options.

Now that you know that it exists, you can examine it for ideas if your business has a need for this type of dashboard. The actual dashboard is too busy with too much going on and should be limited to the top section that can be seen without scrolling. It appears to have been designed primarily to support the static **Intro** tab rather than informing us about investments. Pie charts can often be misleading because of the way humans tend to interpret them, but in this case, the pie chart is visually informative with its color coding matching the column headers. The three small bar graphs underneath often get hidden below the main area on the web page when the web page is displayed at 100 percent — not even enlarged. They don't seem to interact with the central, eye-catching pie chart, so they would be better off having their own tabs in a real environment.

If you have specific questions about this dashboard, you can click on **HELP** in the QlikView interface, and it will set up an e-mail for you to ask your questions. Additional server-based QlikView examples that might also contribute ideas are *Investment Profitability*, *Investment Research*, and *Risk Scenario Analysis*. These, as is the case with **Asset Management** dashboard, are server-based and locked down. Search for them on the QlikView demo site at `http://us-b.demo.qlik.com/`.

Fixed asset management

Before we move into loading outside sources into a QlikView document, we will have a quick look at our definition of *fixed asset management* and how we might want to display that information.

Fixed asset management is the process of tracking fixed assets for the purposes of financial accounting, preventive maintenance, and theft deterrence.

The most commonly tracked assets are the following:

- Plant and equipment
- Buildings
- Fixtures and fittings
- Long-term investment
- Machinery
- Vehicles and heavy equipment
- Computer equipment and peripherals

Displaying a report of an organization's fixed assets would probably best be accomplished with an Excel-type list, similar to the one you can see on the **Investment Screener** tab of the **Asset Management** QlikView document we opened earlier from the Web. Instead of **Funds Available** and the number, we will put summary group values at the top and have an asset-type grouping. Then we can filter on that and change the value and the information. As a suggestion, please review the following screenshot:

| FIXED ASSETS CURRENT VALUE | | $3,210,035 | All Assets | | | | | | | | | | | | | | |
Asset Type	Asset or serial number	Item description (make and model)	Location	Condition	Vendor	Years of Service	Years of service left	Initial value	Down payment	Date purchased or leased	Loan term in years	Loan rate	Monthly payment	Monthly operating costs	Total monthly cost	Expected value at end of loan term	Annual straight line depreciation	Monthly straight line depreciation	Current value
Equipment	123	Cargo Pod	Main branch	good	local	7	5	$ 30,000.00	$ 5,000.00	1/15/2009	4	10.00%	$ 634.06	$ 200.00	$ 634.06	$ 25,000.00	$ 1,250.00	$ 104.17	21,337.79
Building	125	Main branch	Main branch	good	N/A	30	20	$ 2,500,000.00	$ 500,000.00	1/30/2001	30	0.06%	$ 5,604.16	$5,000.00	$ 10,604.16	$ 4,000,000.00	$ (50,000.00)	$ (4,166.67)	3,194,570.44
Computer	126	Server HP 7500	Main branch	good	HP	5	3	$ 10,000.00	$ 1,000.00	4/19/2009	4	0.08%	$ 187.91	$ 60.00	$ 247.91	$ -	$ 2,500.00	$ 208.33	(6,680.59)
Computer	127	Server Dell 2600	Main branch	good	Dell	5	3	$ 12,000.00	$ 1,200.00	7/23/2009	4	0.07%	$ 225.32	$ 60.00	$ 285.32	$ -	$ 3,000.00	$ 250.00	(7,227.65)
Equipment	123	Truck	Main branch	good	NC2	7	5	$ 30,000.00	$ 5,000.00	1/15/2009	4	10.00%	$ 634.06	$ 200.00	$ 634.06	$ 25,000.00	$ 1,250.00	$ 104.17	21,337.79
Computer	127	Server Dell 2600	Main branch	good	Dell	5	3	$ 12,000.00	$ 1,200.00	7/23/2009	4	0.07%	$ 225.32	$ 60.00	$ 285.32	$ -	$ 3,000.00	$ 250.00	(7,227.65)
Computer	126	Server HP 7500	Main branch	good	HP	5	3	$ 10,000.00	$ 1,000.00	4/18/2009	4	0.08%	$ 187.91	$ 60.00	$ 247.91	$ -	$ 2,500.00	$ 208.33	(6,680.59)
Computer	127	Server Dell 2600	Main branch	good	Dell	5	3	$ 12,000.00	$ 1,200.00	7/23/2009	4	0.07%	$ 225.32	$ 60.00	$ 285.32	$ -	$ 3,000.00	$ 250.00	(7,227.65)
Equipment	123	Truck	Main branch	good	NC2	7	5	$ 30,000.00	$ 5,000.00	1/15/2009	4	10.00%	$ 634.06	$ 200.00	$ 634.06	$ 25,000.00	$ 1,250.00	$ 104.17	21,337.79
Computer	127	Server Dell 2600	Main branch	good	Dell	5	3	$ 12,000.00	$ 1,200.00	7/23/2009	4	0.07%	$ 225.32	$ 60.00	$ 285.32	$ -	$ 3,000.00	$ 250.00	(7,227.65)
Computer	126	Server HP 7500	Main branch	good	HP	5	3	$ 10,000.00	$ 1,000.00	4/18/2009	4	0.08%	$ 187.91	$ 60.00	$ 247.91	$ -	$ 2,500.00	$ 208.33	(6,680.59)
Computer	127	Server Dell 2600	Main branch	good	Dell	5	3	$ 12,000.00	$ 1,200.00	7/23/2009	4	0.07%	$ 225.32	$ 60.00	$ 285.32	$ -	$ 3,000.00	$ 250.00	(7,227.65)
Equipment	123	Truck	Main branch	good	NC2	7	5	$ 30,000.00	$ 5,000.00	1/15/2009	4	10.00%	$ 634.06	$ 200.00	$ 634.06	$ 25,000.00	$ 1,250.00	$ 104.17	21,337.79
Computer	127	Server Dell 2600	Main branch	good	Dell	5	3	$ 12,000.00	$ 1,200.00	7/23/2009	4	0.07%	$ 225.32	$ 60.00	$ 285.32	$ -	$ 3,000.00	$ 250.00	(7,227.65)
Computer	126	Server HP 7500	Main branch	good	HP	5	3	$ 10,000.00	$ 1,000.00	4/19/2009	4	0.08%	$ 187.91	$ 60.00	$ 247.91	$ -	$ 2,500.00	$ 208.33	(6,680.59)
Computer	127	Server Dell 2600	Main branch	good	Dell	5	3	$ 12,000.00	$ 1,200.00	7/23/2009	4	0.07%	$ 225.32	$ 60.00	$ 285.32	$ -	$ 3,000.00	$ 250.00	(7,227.65)
Equipment	123	Truck	Main branch	good	NC2	7	5	$ 30,000.00	$ 5,000.00	1/15/2009	4	10.00%	$ 634.06	$ 200.00	$ 634.06	$ 25,000.00	$ 1,250.00	$ 104.17	21,337.79

Figure 4-2: Fixed asset-tracking display example

Organizations face a significant challenge to track the location, quantity, condition, maintenance, and depreciation status of their fixed assets. A popular approach to tracking fixed assets uses serial-numbered asset tags with bar codes for easy and accurate reading. Periodically, the owner of the assets can take an inventory with a mobile bar code reader and then produce a report. Ideally, that report should be exportable in an electronic format that could then be imported into QlikView for reporting and budgeting replacement assets. The next section of this chapter will demonstrate what the script sections look like for several different sources that can be imported into a QlikView document.

Adding data sources

Now, reopen `Executive Dashboard.qvw` in the examples. Choose **File | Edit Script**.

Loading from another QlikView document

Although there is not much left to learn from the actual scripts in the CFO executive dashboard, we can see from the very first statement in the script that we are loading from another QlikView document with the same name em dash except with lowercase letters. The following is the first statement in the script:

```
Binary [executive dashboard.qvw];
```

The binary statement is used for loading the data from another QlikView document. It does not load the layout information or variables. Only one binary statement is allowed in the script, and it can only be put as the first statement of a script. You can use relative locations, and there is a checkbox to get QlikView to generate a relative location statement. This allows you to move your QlikView operations to folders on another computer or another server without extensive editing of script load paths.

Loading from files

At the bottom of the script interface, we find the area where we can load more data of different types. Using the wizard for all the different *Table* files at the bottom of the script allows QlikView to build the script for you. You will not have to edit the script unless you want to rename the fields. But learning what a script for a particular type of file looks like can be helpful in analyzing what someone else has done. It can even assist you in adjusting your data loads to meet your needs.

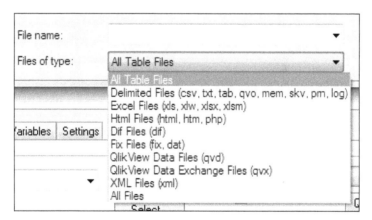

Figure 4-3: File types for loading

QlikView files

Here, we see that we can load other QlikView files by saving them as **QlikView Data Files** and **QlikView Exchange Files**. So we are not truly limited to one QlikView file, that is, one of the document (.qvw) type. A QlikView Data (QVD) file is a file containing a table of data exported from QlikView. QVD is a native QlikView format and can only be written to and read by QlikView. QVX, the exchange file format, is a stream or text file for high-performance input and output from QlikView.

The following are three examples of how the load script section for loading from a QVD file might appear. Notice that in the third load example, we will be renaming our dimension fields a, b, and c:

```
load * from myAssets.qvd (qvd);
load AssetNo, AssetDesc, AssetValue from myAssets.qvd (qvd);
load AssetNo as a, AssetDesc as b, AssetValue as c from myAssets.qvd
(qvd);
```

Here is a more complicated example from the *Sales Compass* example QlikView document. It shows loads from the system date and a QVD file with links to other QVD files being loaded in other sections of the script, previously declared variables, and load date variables. The opening LinkTable: declaration creates a new table from the data loaded from the other sources so that it can be handled more quickly by QlikView. This is known as a *Resident Table*. The declaration must precede any statements loading the table, and the load section ends with the Resident statement:

```
LinkTable:
LOAD DISTINCT
   Year(Date) as Year,
   Month(Date) as Month,
   Date(MonthStart(Date), 'MMMYY') as MonthYear,
   if(monthstart(Date) <= $(vTodaysDate), 1, 0) as _History,
   'Q' & Ceil(Month(Date)/3) as Quarter,
   Dual('Q' & Ceil(Month(Date)/3) & '-' & Year(Date), Year(Date) &
Ceil(Month(Date)/3)) as QtrYear,
   Week(Date) as Week,
   Weekstart(Date) as Weekstart,
   Weekend(Date) as Weekend
   ;
Load
   Date($(vEndDate) - RecNo() +1) as Date
AutoGenerate($(NumberOfDays));

JOIN LOAD DISTINCT
   text([Customer Number]) as [Customer Number]
```

```
FROM ..\Database\QVDs\Customers.qvd (qvd);

JOIN LOAD DISTINCT
  [Address Number] as [Customer Number],
  Year([Invoice Date]) as Year,
  [Sales Rep Number]
RESIDENT Sales;

DROP FIELD [Sales Rep Number] FROM Sales;


LEFT JOIN LOAD
  MonthYear,
  [Customer Number],
  date(MonthYear) & '_' & [Customer Number] as BudgetKey,
  date(MonthYear) & '_' & [Customer Number] & '_' & [Sales Rep Number]
as SalesKey,
  date(MonthYear) & '_' & [Sales Rep Number] as QuotaKey
RESIDENT LinkTable;
```

XML files

We can load from XML format files, such as an exchange rate sample file, from `http://www.ex.com`. Ex.com is one of many companies specializing in supplying foreign exchange rates on a periodic basis (hourly, daily, or monthly) for a fee. An XML load script will look similar to the following:

```
// Start of [sample-xml-usd.xml] LOAD statements
header:
LOAD hname,
  hvalue
FROM [C:\TEST\sample-xml-usd.xml] (XmlSimple, Table is [xe-datafeed/
header]);

currency:
LOAD csymbol,
  cname,
  crate,
  cinverse
FROM [C:\Test\sample-xml-usd.xml] (XmlSimple, Table is [xe-datafeed/
currency]);
// End of [sample-xml-usd.xml] LOAD statements
```

HTML files

HTML web files can be loaded from websites to add information to a QlikView document. An HTML script will look similar to the following script. Notice how we are able to name our incoming data columns and do mathematical changes to the incoming data in the body of the script:

```
// Example of loading from an HTML type file. The ranks in this file
need to be reversed as they are an average of the other fields.
Original data source - Reader's Digest magazine on line.
LOAD upper(F1) as City,
    F2 as Air,
    F3 as Water,
    F4 as Toxics,
    F5 as Hazard_Waste,
    F6 as Sanitation,
    F7*(-1)+51 as Rank,
    F2*(-1)+51 as Air_Quality,
    F3*(-1)+51 as Water_Quality
    FROM
[C:\TEST\50 Cleanest Cities in America Reader's Digest.mht]
(html, codepage is 1252, embedded labels, table is @1);
```

In addition to loading HTML files through the file interface, you can also use the **Web Files** button to connect to and load a file from the Internet.

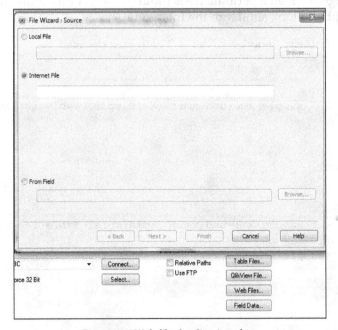

Figure 4-4: Web files loading interface

A web document-generated load script will look similar to the following example:

```
LOAD [e-mail us at webmaster@blackwood.org]
FROM
[http://www.blackwood.org]
(html, codepage is 1252, embedded labels, table is @1, filters(
ColSplit(1, IntArray())
));
```

Excel files

We already know from earlier chapters that we can load from Excel, but the different versions will look slightly different in the scripting. For example, when loading from an Excel 2010 file, two different sheets are used with similar data. Rank is set as a measure, and City is converted to uppercase and is a dimension in the following script example.

State is also a dimension. Because City and State are named the same in the two worksheets, they automatically join:

```
LOAD Rank,
    UPPER(City) as City,
    State,
    Hospital_Quality as Health_Care
FROM
C:\TEST\NaturalDisasterRank.xlsx
(ooxml, embedded labels, table is HealthCare);

LOAD Rank,
    Upper(City) as City,
    Average,
    Water_Quality,
    [Heat stress],
    [Natural disaster risk] as Low_Natural_Hazard,
    State
FROM
C:\TEST\NaturalDisasterRank.xlsx
(ooxml, embedded labels, table is NAT_DIS);

    // Loading from an Excel 2003 file
LOAD UPPER(City) as City,
    State,
    Zipcode,
    KnowSomeone as Near_Friends,
    1 as Rank
```

```
FROM
[C:\TEST\Cities Personal List1.xls]
(biff, embedded labels, table is Personal$);
```

Loading from an Excel 2003 file will use the file extension `.xls` instead of the newer `.xlsx` file extension. It is labeled as a `biff` internal format instead of `ooxml`. Notice that internal comments can be added to scripts with the double forward slashes that you see in front of the statement: `Loading from an Excel 2003 file`.

Text and delimited files

In addition to Excel files, almost all delimited export-type files are supported, including tab-delimited and comma-separated values.

Loading from databases

We have not exhausted the possible sources for loading to a QlikView document. Any database that we can connect to with an ODBC connection, an OLE DB connection, or a QlikView server connection can be a source to load QlikView from. It is also possible to use **File Transfer Protocol (FTP)** to extract the data from a file to one of the text or delimited file formats.

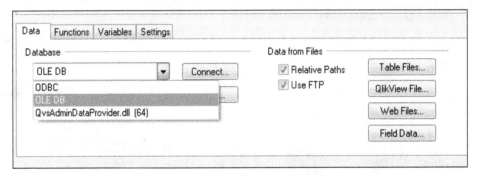

Figure 4-5: Database connection types

Next, we have two examples of what the script looks like when loading from ODBC data sources. The first is a connection to an SQL server (which happens to be named SQL Server), and the second is a connection to a Microsoft Access database:

```
// Loading from a SQL Server database
ODBC CONNECT TO SQL_Server;
LOAD "Avg_Ticket_Price",
  UPPER (City) as City,
  "Online_Tickets",
  Rank,
```

```
    Screens,
    State,
    Theaters,
    Rank as Entertainment;
SQL SELECT "Avg_Ticket_Price",
    City,
    "Online_Tickets",
    Rank,
    Screens,
    State,
    Theaters,
    Rank as Entertainment
FROM AdventureWorks.dbo."US_Theaters";

// Loading from an Access database via ODBC
ODBC CONNECT TO [MS Access Database;DBQ=C:\TEST\greatplaces.mdb];
LOAD DISTINCT UPPER (City) as City,
    ID,
    State,
    Rank,
    Zip;
SQL SELECT City,
    ID,
    State,
    Rank,
    Zip,
    1 as Cost_of_Living
FROM `MLS_List`;
```

Summary

Knowing that there are so many sources of data to analyse that can be loaded into QlikView can give a sense of great power. We can load asset management information from files, database data sources, and the Internet. We examined the **QlikView Asset Management** dashboard example. We found that there are many other sources of ideas to create a whole dashboard or just a tab that can be used for the type of asset management that best suits our business needs.

Now that we know that our data sources are nearly limitless, in the next chapter, we will look at more charts reporting sales, ideas for displaying tables, and how the examples are created.

5
QlikView Sales Analysis

We now return to the Executive dashboard that we used in *Chapter 3, KPIs in the Financial Officer QlikView Dashboard*.

In this chapter, we will cover the example QlikView CFO dashboard — **Sales Analysis** tab:

- The good, the bad, and the ugly — the display of the **Sales Analysis** tab
- The nuts and bolts of the **Sales Analysis** tab
- Creating a better version from the existing version of the **Sales Analysis** tab

Reopening the example CFO dashboard

We are going to review the **Sales Analysis** tab of the `Executive Dashboard.qvw` from the examples we downloaded when we installed QlikView. If it is not open, please open it now and navigate to the **Sales Analysis** tab:

1. Open QlikView if it is not open already.
2. Using the **File | Open** menu in QlikView, navigate to the **Program Files | QlikView | Examples | Documents** folder, and double-click on the `Executive Dashboard.qvw` file to open it.
3. Select the fourth tab: the **Sales Analysis** tab.

4. The screen will look similar to the following screenshot:

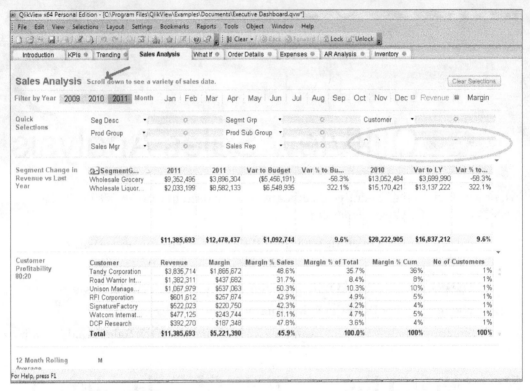

Figure 5-1: The upper half of the Sales Analysis sheet in the Executive dashboard

The sales analysis tab in a nutshell

The **Sales Analysis** tab has many poor display choices and some good ones. Too much information is crammed onto the sheet. Although the months and years are readily visible, thus inviting selections and matching the display of the KPIs tab so that there is continuity between sheets, the sheet does require scrolling to see the chart images at the bottom of the display. People tend to assume that, if scrolling is necessary, the information that is out of sight is of less importance than the information that is readily visible. The goal is to provide readily actionable information that is easy to see and understand. The designer has tried to mitigate this problem by adding text indicating that we need to scroll down the sheet (see the arrow near the top-left corner of the preceding screenshot), but that is generally considered a poor design choice.

Also, the spacing of the eight **Quick Selections** is incorrect, and we cannot see the name next to the quick selection bar for **Country** (see the oval near the top-right corner).

The table display

There are two straight tables displayed in the top half of the sheet:

- **Segment Change in Revenue vs Last Year**
- **Customer Profitability 80:20**

The first, **Segment Change**, has eight columns of data. The second, **Customer Profitability**, only has six but requires intensive scrolling to see the data by customer. In both tables, the data is displayed out to the 1 dollar unit rather than being rounded up to thousands or millions. This leads to the hard work of remembering and comparing numbers to figure out what is important in the information. Unfortunately, there is no quick way to change the display in QlikView between ones, thousands, and millions.

The chart display

Once we scroll down the page to the chart display, we see two charts displaying basically identical information. The first shows a rolling 12-month average sales and margin % in line graph format. The second is a bar chart with the gross sales and margin that has a line graph going across the top of **Margin** %. Also, the "12 month" name of the first graph is a misnomer because there is only enough data to display 7 months of 2010 and 5 months of 2011, and only one year of data appears at a time with the default selection. You must choose both 2010 and 2011 to get 12 months to be displayed at the same time in the **12 Month Rolling Average** line graph. To choose both years, hold down the *Shift* key and click each year in turn. And when you do select both years, **Monthly Sales & Margin** does not display the same comparison time period and doesn't tell us which year we are viewing.

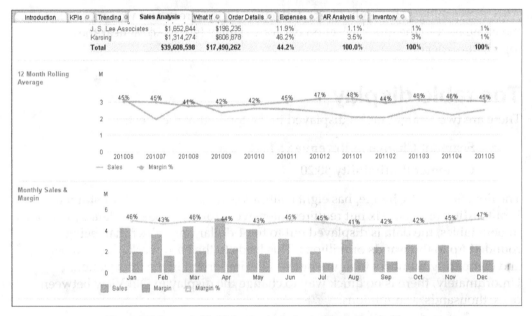

Figure 5-2: Lower half of Sales Analysis sheet of Executive dashboard

The nuts and bolts of the sales analysis dashboard

We will now start looking at the components that make up the **Sales Analysis** dashboard so that we can leverage them to make improvements.

The group button

Although the text title on the left-hand side of the straight table (**Segment Change in Revenue vs Last Year**) does not change, you can change what is displayed in the straight table, **Segment Changes in Revenue**, using the **Group** button in the upper left corner of the table (see *Figure 5-3*):

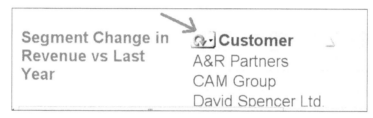

Figure 5-3: The Dimension Selection button in the straight table

This button looks like a circular arrow; if you hover over it, the word **Cycle** pops up in a box. The button allows you to scroll through group measures selected for the table. Provided at least two or more expressions are available to create a group, the **Group** button can be used in transforming merged group expressions of dimensions or measures into one or more cyclic groups.

In the QlikView layout, you can cycle through the expressions belonging to one group by clicking on the cycle icon that is displayed in the chart (cycle group). Right-click on the same cycle icon to get a pop-up list of the expressions belonging to the group that are currently unused for direct selection.

To investigate, change or add a group to the **Changes in Revenue** straight table.

1. Right-click and choose **Properties**.
2. Click on the **Dimensions** tab.

3. In the lower-left corner of the **Dimensions** tab, click on the **Edit Groups** button.

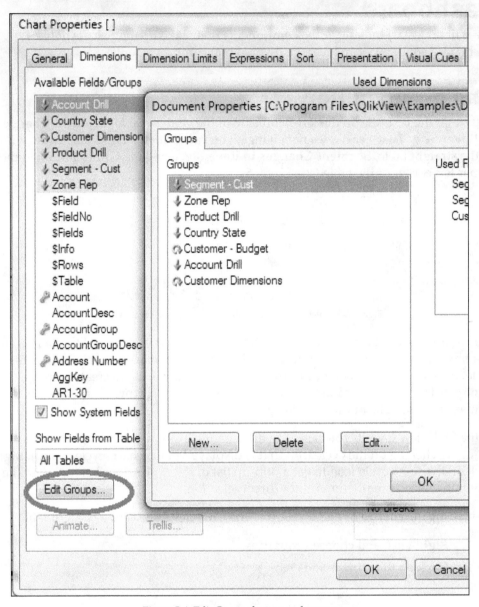

Figure 5-4: Edit Groups button and popup

4. In the new pop-up screen in the lower-left corner, click on the **New** button to create a new group.

5. Name your group `Total Group`.

6. Using the **Add** button, move several dimensions into the group, such as:

    ° **Customer**

    ° **Product Group Desc**

    ° **Business Family**

    ° **Customer Type**

    ° **Product Sub Group Desc**

7. Make sure you switch the radio button at the top from **Drill-down Group** to **Cyclic Group**.

8. Click on the **OK** button.

9. Click on the next **OK** button.

10. Move the new group that you created to **Used Dimensions** with the **Add** button.

11. Click on the **OK** button to close the wizard, and add your new group to the table.

Notice how your new cyclic group is now in the straight table inside the other cyclic group. Experiment with how selections in one group affect the other and how selections in multi-boxes in containers affect both groups.

 At this point, you can choose to save `Executive Dashboard` as a new QlikView document with a different name. I chose `Executive Dashboard - Diane`. You still will not be able to reload the script because you do not have access to the QlikView server, but you can save your changes to the sheet objects this way.

Containers

Now, we will examine the larger components of the **Sales Analysis** dashboard. Start by clicking on the sheet in a vacant area and choosing **Properties**. Then, navigate to the **Objects** tab. Here, we can see all objects that make up the sheet and their IDs, Types, and other properties.

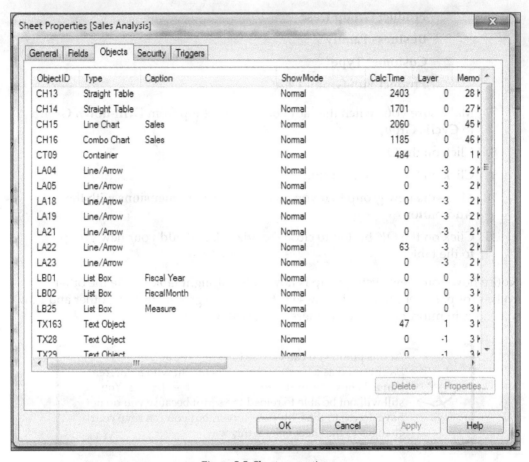

Figure 5-5: Sheet properties

Click on a specific row in the tab, and it will activate the two buttons, **Delete** and **Properties**, in the lower-right corner of the wizard. If you click on the **Delete** button, it will actually delete the object from the sheet. If you click on the **Properties** button, it will pop up another wizard with the ability to edit the properties for the object you selected.

Here, we can see that we have two straight tables, one line chart, one combo chart, one container object, and multiple other formatting and informational objects.

1. Click on the container object line. It is labeled **CT09**.

2. Now, click on the **Properties** button.

You will now see the **Properties** box for the container object; it shows that container object contains eight multi box objects.

Multi boxes in a container allow us to further filter our data. As noted before, the spacing is not quite right inside the container, and we cannot see the multi box or its label for **Country**. You can still click on it and choose a country as a filter, but it is difficult to see.

Now, we will add the container to the right-hand side of the **Sales Analysis** sheet.

1. Right-click on the empty area of the sheet and choose **New Sheet Object...**

2. Choose the container, and name the container if you wish. Click on **OK**.

3. A new container appears on the sheet.

4. Now, right-click on your new container and choose **Properties**.

5. Using the **Add** button, move **TX174** (a text box) and **CH56 Age Profile** (a chart) into your container.

6. Click **OK**.

Size the container with the mouse and white-filled, double-ended arrows by hovering near a container edge, and then by left-clicking when you get the arrow. It is actually easiest to move your container by changing the size. Now, you see what looks like one object on the sheet, a tiny letter **A** in a gray box, and another gray box that says **Age Profile** and shows a pie chart and key, as shown in the following screenshot:

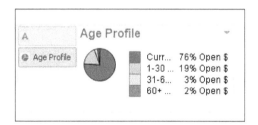

Figure 5-6: New objects in the container

 Actually, the **Age Profile** chart is related to accounts receivable aging, and you can see the full object on the **AR Analysis** tab that we will analyze in a later chapter.

If we click on **A** in our new container, the chart image is replaced by a giant picture of the word **QlikView**, which is so big that only part of the image can be seen. If we now click on the **Age Profile** button in our new container, the display returns to the pie chart. If we click on the **Age Profile** key or an area in the pie chart in our new container, the pie chart goes to the first key color displaying a single circle, and the one key item selected now changes to **100**%. Too bad there isn't an easy way to change the pie chart to retain the key and key color change when selected. Perhaps, we could use something like alternating visibility charts, such as the ones used on the **KPIs** tab. We leave that exercise to you. Interestingly, nothing on the **AR Analysis** tab seems linked to this chart but, by adding the **Age Profile** chart to the **Sales Analysis** tab, we can filter data in both straight tables readily visible in the top half of the screen. Also, clicking on the pie chart a second time returns it to the original multi-slice display.

If we navigate to the **Customer Profitability** straight table and click on the customer, **J.S. Lee Associates**, our display changes, and **J.S. Lee Associates** now shows up in the multi box for **Customer**. Also, the pie chart in **Aging Profile** switches to show two keys that tell us that this customer has accounts receivable falling into two categories, current and between 1 and 30 days past due. That is very interesting information, but we might be better served if we created a new tab for **Customer Profitability**, where we could investigate this kind of information without interfering with **Sales Analysis**.

Improving the sales analysis dashboard

Instead of spreading out our data to the point where we have information overload, perhaps we could remove a few objects and produce a better dashboard? I experimented by saving `Executive Dashboard` under a new name. Then, I made a copy of the **Sales Analysis** dashboard and started editing.

[To make a copy of a sheet, right-click on the sheet that you want to copy in a vacant area and choose **Copy Sheet**.]

When I finished, my new sheet, **Copy of Sales Analysis**, looked like the following screenshot:

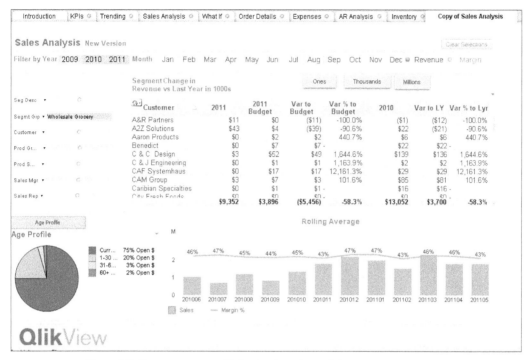

Figure 5-7: The new version of Sales Analysis sheet of the Executive dashboard

I chose to move the **Customer Profitability** table to its own tab because, although it is related to **Sales**, it is really a separate investigation and thought process. Either graph is acceptable, but I chose to keep **Rolling Average Sales to Margin** since it does show the year and month for the data represented. I moved the multi box group to the side, where the titles are not hidden. If we wanted to filter by those same items, we could put the cyclic group back into the straight table and get rid of the multi boxes. However, multi boxes do tell us whether we have a specific filter applied and take advantage of the relationship features of QlikView to tell us which other items are related.

Steps to create a new sales analysis tab

If you have not done so already, save a personal copy of `Executive Dashboard`.

 Save your `Executive Dashboard` as a new QlikView document with a different name using **File | Save as...** so that you can return to it at your convenience.

Perform the following steps to create a new **Sales Analysis** tab:

1. Click on the **File** menu and then choose **Save As...**

2. Save your new personal copy under a folder that you have access to and with a name you will remember. It will show up in the list of **Recents** when you start QlikView the next time.

3. Now, copy the **Sales Analysis** tab. Right-click on a vacant area of the **Sales Analysis** sheet to bring up the context menu, and choose **Copy Sheet ...**

4. Now, start cleaning up the new sheet. Right-click on the **Customer Profitability** straight table and, from the pop-up context menu, choose **Remove**. Verify that you really want to remove the object. Do the same for the text box that has the informational title.

5. Next, remove the container with multi boxes as we will recreate it in a different step and as it is taking up valuable screen real estate without being easily seen

    1. Right-click and choose **Properties** for the container. Make sure you have the **CT09** container and not the new one you created. Remove all multi boxes from the container by moving them back to the existing objects with the **Remove** button.

    2. Click on **OK** to see the empty container.

    3. Now, right-click on the empty container and choose **Remove**.

    4. Verify that you want to remove the container.

    5. Click the **Undo Layout** button, or choose **Undo Layout** under the **Edit** menu, if you make a mistake.

6. In order to move objects remaining on the sheet or resize them, we must enable the **Allow Move/Size** property. Start with the **Line/Arrow** object that was underneath the container that we deleted:

    1. Right-click on the **Line/Arrow** object and choose **Properties**.

    2. Navigate to the **Layout** tab of the wizard.

    3. Go to the **Options** section on the **Layout** tab (mid-right) and click on the **Allow Move/Size** checkbox.

4. Click on **Apply** at the bottom of the wizard, and click on **OK** to close.

5. Now, move the line up under the **Year/Month/Revenue – Margin** row.

6. Repeat as needed to enable the moving of objects on the page.

7. To lock an item in place, uncheck **Allow Move/Size**.

7. Enable **Move/Size** on the **Segment Change vs Revenue vs Last Year** title and move it up under the word **Month**—just under the line you moved previously.

8. Now, resize the title to two lines. Hover and use the white-filled double-ended arrow to resize text box.

9. Next, enable **Move/Size** on the **Layout** tab for the straight table **CH63**—the one associated with the **Segment** title.

10. While we are in the wizard for the straight table, let's change the table column headers. In the **Multiline Setting** section on the **Presentation** tab in the lower-right corner, check the box for **Wrap Header Text**, and leave the default to two lines. Click on **OK**.

11. Click on **OK** again to exit the wizard, and then hover over the white space above and below the **CH63** straight table. Stretch it under the title.

12. Now, we are going to create the ability to switch our numbers in the straight table from ones to thousands and then to millions.

Creating a new variable

Perform the following steps to create a new variable:

1. Go to the **Settings** menu at the top and choose **Document Properties**.

2. Navigate to the **Variables** tab.

3. Click on **New** to add a new variable. Name your new variable vNumDisplay.

4. Under **Settings** for the selected variable section (in the lower-left corner) in the **Value** field, enter **1000** as the default value. Leave the rest of the defaults, and click on **OK** to exit the **Settings** wizard.

An interface for the new variable

1. Create a new sheet object. Right-click to bring up the context menu and choose **New Sheet Object...**, and then choose **Text Object**.

2. In the **Text** field on the **General** tab, type the word Millions.

3. On the **Actions** tab, click on the **Add** button. Choose the **External for Action** type and choose **Set Variable for Action**.

4. Click on the ellipses (**...**) next to the **Variables** box, and navigate to the **Variables** tab in the **Edit Expression** wizard that pops up. Choose our new **vNumDisplay** variable, and click on paste to put it into the **Expression** box.

5. In the **Value** box, type 1000000 to set the value.

6. Now, click on **OK** to exit the wizard. Size your new text object, move it above the table, and line it up below **Dec**.

7. Repeat steps 1 through 6 to create new text objects for ones (enter 1 in the **Value** box), and move them under the word **Aug**. For thousands, enter 1000 in the **Value** box and move the new text objects under the word **Oct**.

8. We have now created three button-type objects to interface with other objects on our sheet.

 If you have difficulty getting the ones box to activate, make sure it is not overlapped by the **Segment** title text object.

Applying the new variable

1. Now we need to edit the expressions in our **CH63** straight table to use text boxes to apply our variables:

    1. Right-click on the **Straight Table** and choose **Properties**.

    2. Navigate to the **Expressions** tab.

    3. Starting with the expression (the first one) $(vCurrentYear), click on the ellipses (**...**) next to **Definition** (right-hand side, third object from the bottom).

    4. Now, edit the expression by typing / to indicate that we are dividing.

    5. Then, go to the **Variables** tab in the **Edit Expression** wizard, and navigate to the new **vNumDisplay** variable. Click on **Paste** to paste our new variable onto the expression behind the forward slash (virgule). Our expression should now look like this:

       ```
       Sum({<[Fiscal Year]={$(vCurrentYear)}>}[Sales Amount])/
       vNumDisplay
       ```

6. For the expression (the second one) $(vCurrentYear), click on the ellipses (...) next to **Definition** (the right-hand side, the third object from the bottom).

7. Now, edit the expression by typing / to indicate we are dividing.

8. Then, go to the **Variables** tab in the **Edit Expression** wizard, and navigate to our new variable **vNumDisplay**. Paste our new variable onto the expression behind the forward slash. Our expression should now look similar to this:

```
Sum ([Budget Amount])/vNumDisplay
```

9. Before we leave this expression, let's clarify in the table header that we are looking at the budget for the current year. In the **Label** box, just above **Expression Definition**, click on the ellipses (...) to bring up the **Edit Expression** wizard. In the **Expression** box, type **Budget** and then click on **OK** to close.

10. Finally, let's add our variable to the prior year's expression. Click on the expression $(=(vCurrentYear)-1) to select it.

11. Edit **Definition** by adding / and our variable **vNumDisplay**. Our expression should now look similar to this:

```
Sum({<[Fiscal Year]={$(=(vCurrentYear)-1)}>}[Sales Amount])/
vNumDisplay
```

2. Click on **OK** to exit.

The straight table (**CH63**) now displays thousands as the default, but we cannot tell just by looking what precision is being displayed in our table—ones, thousands, or millions. To change that, edit the text box (**TX180**) title that we moved up earlier. Add a space after the word in and before the final apostrophe. Then, add an ampersand (&) and a space. Type in the name of our variable and another space followed by another ampersand. Finally, type in an apostrophe followed by an s and then another apostrophe. The expression will look similar to this:

```
='Segment Change in' & chr(10) & 'Revenue vs Last Year in '  &
vNumDisplay & 's'
```

Now, when we click on our boxes, the title will change to indicate the precision of our numbers:

Segment Change in Revenue vs Last Year in 1000s					Ones	Thousands	Millions	
SegmentGroup	2011	2011 Budget	Var to Budget	Var % to Budget	2010		Var to LY	Var % to Lyr
Wholesale Grocery	$9,352	$3,896	($5,456)	-58.3%	$13,052		$3,700	-58.3%
Wholesale Liquor...	$2,033	$8,582	$6,549	322.1%	$15,170		$13,137	322.1%
	$0	$7,893	$7,893 -		$0		$0 -	
	$11,386	$20,372	$8,986	78.9%	$28,223		$16,837	78.9%

Figure 5-8: Buttons with thousands as the default and showing in the title

Adding a container with multi boxes

Right-click on a vacant area of the sheet, choose **New Sheet Object** , and then choose Container. To add a container with multi boxes, perform the following steps:

1. Add multi boxes **MB01, MB02, MB03, MB04, MB05, MB09**, and **MB10** to the container on the **General** tab.

2. On the **Presentation** tab, set **Container Type** to **Grid**.

3. Now, set **Columns** to 1 and **Rows** to 7.

4. Size the container into approximately a 2-inch by 2-inch square.

5. Edit each multi box in the container and reduce the font size to **8**.

6. Move the container to the left-hand side of the straight table and size the container to fit.

7. Next, resize the left-hand side and right-hand side of the multi box selection display bar by hovering until you get a black cross (the cross is a double-ended arrow). When it is used on the left-hand side, we can move the rectangular box closer to the title; when it is used on the right-hand side, we can reduce the width of the rectangular box.

8. Now, adjust the size of container again for the best display.

Figure 5-9: Container with Multi Box selection

Moving and changing the chart

To move and change the chart, perform the following steps:

1. Edit the **Line/Arrow** that comes next so that you can move it up and then move it under the straight table.

2. Now, edit the line graph so that it will allow you to move it and then move it under the line you moved previously.

3. Right-click on the moved line graph and, on the **General** tab, check the checkbox labelled **Use Title in Chart**. In the box below that, type **Rolling Average**. On the same tab, change **Chart Type** to **Combo Chart**.

4. Move to the **Expressions** tab. Make sure that you have **Sales** highlighted, and then change **Display Option** from **Line** to **Bar**. Click on **OK** to exit the wizard.

Finally, delete any other objects that you don't want on your sheet. If you want to investigate other possibilities on your own, add back objects in the container and move it into position on the left-hand side of the line graph. After the container is in place and sized, use the **Properties** wizard to insert the **Age Profile Chart** object.

To make the **Ones**, **Thousands**, and **Millions** boxes look more like buttons, try adding shadow borders.

Summary

We examined the **Sales Analysis** dashboard (the existing one) and the good and bad choices made in the display. You learned how to create a **Group** button to make more data available on a single display without overcrowding or overloading information for the user of the dashboard.

We created a new **Sales Analysis** dashboard tab organized into a better visual layout using the exact same data as in the original dashboard.

While doing this, you learned how to create a toggle for the numbers displayed, so that it is easier to compare them and easier to remember how they compare for further investigation. We did this by creating a variable and text boxes to assign values to the variable. Then, we used the variable in our formulas to display our data.

We rearranged and changed the original objects for a meaningful display.

You learned about containers and how to remove them and the objects inside. We also created new containers and put objects in those containers.

In the next chapter, we will examine the **What If** tab of the **Executive** dashboard for ideas on forecasting.

6
QlikView Forecasting and Trends

In this chapter, we will cover several of the QlikView tabs in the example CFO dashboard for ideas to use in forecasting and examining trends:

- How to create a trend line or extend a forecast line in **Charts** using the **Sales Analysis** tab
- The nuts and bolts of the **Trending** tab
- The nuts and bolts of the **What If?** tab

Being able to predict likely future business scenarios by examining forecasts and trends can help us manage our business and quickly see whether there are steps that we can take to improve business profits.

Reopening the example CFO dashboard

We are going to start with the **Sales Analysis** sheet of Executive Dashboard.qvw from the examples we downloaded when we installed QlikView. If it is not open, please open it now, and navigate to the **Sales Analysis** tab:

1. Open QlikView if it is not open already.
2. Using the **File | Open** menu in QlikView, navigate to the **Program Files | QlikView | Examples | Documents** folder and double-click on Executive Dashboard.qvw to open it.
3. Select the fourth tab: the **Sales Analysis** tab.
4. Scroll down to the **Charts** displayed at the bottom of the tab.

Trend and forecast lines in charts

We will start by adding a trend line to the lower chart, **Monthly Sales and Margin**. Then, we will add a forecasted trend line out 3 months to the upper chart, with a 12-month rolling average.

Adding a trend line to the monthly sales and margin chart

1. Right-click on the chart titled **Monthly Sales and Margin** and choose **Properties**:

2. Navigate to the **Dimensions** tab.

3. Click on the **Add** button to add a new dimension.

4. On the right-hand side in the **Label** box, type the word Trend.

5. Next, click on the ellipses to enter the formula for our trend line:

    ```
    if(v12month<=month(today()),sum({<YYYYMM ={">$(v12month)"}>}[Sales
    Amount]),avg(total aggr(if(v12month<=month(today()),sum([Sales
    Amount])),v12month)))
    ```

    Our formula says that, if the variable in v12month is less than the current month, then use the sum of the data we have in Sales Amount. If we don't have the current month's data, then get an average of the aggregate of the last 12 months of data:

6. Make sure that the checkbox is checked and *not* the bar.

7. Click on **Apply** and then click on **OK**.

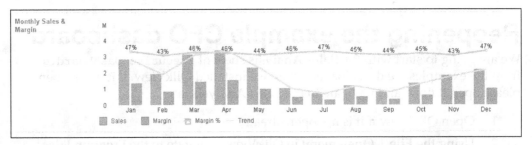

Figure 6-1: Lower half of the Sales Analysis sheet of the Executive dashboard with trend lines

Notice how the trend line has been added to the chart and to the key across the bottom. Hovering with the mouse pointer over the trend line on the right-hand side of the taller red bars will display the exact number that the trend calculation produced.

Open the **Properties** wizard again. Now navigate to the **Style** tab where you can see a color preview of the chart with the yellow trend line added.

Next, go to the **Colors** tab. This is where the colors of our chart items are coming from. The left-hand side shows each color in our chart in a row.

1. Click on the first colored rectangle to change the color used for the first item.

2. When the **Color Area** wizard pops up, click on the rectangle in the upper-right corner and not the preview box in the centre-left.

3. Choose a different color from the **Color Picker**.

4. Click on **OK** to exit the **Color Picker**.

5. Click on **OK** to exit the **Advanced Color Map**.

6. Click on **OK** again to exit the **Properties** wizard.

Be patient as it may take a minute to make the switch and refresh the dialog contents:

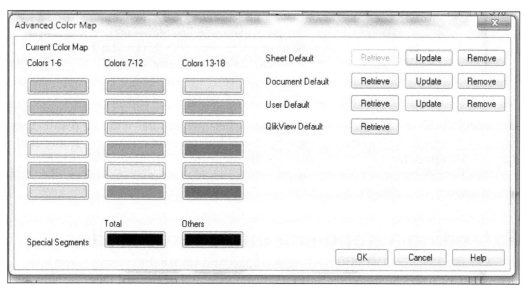

Figure 6-2: The Advanced Color Map interface

In the **Advanced Color Map** interface of the **Properties** wizard, you may have noticed that you can have **Sheet Default**, **Document Default**, **User Default**, and **QlikView Default**. User associated defaults allow us to tailor our dashboards to specific colors for those people with a color vision deficiency. **Colors** can also be set via formulas and themes, which we will examine in the later section on the **Trending** tab.

Basing a trend line on an existing measure

1. Now, right-click on the chart titled **12 Month Rolling Average** and choose **Properties**.

2. Navigate directly to the **Expressions** tab.

3. Click on the expression named **Sales** in the box in the upper-left corner.

4. Notice the box in the lower-left corner that is labelled **Trend Lines**.

5. Now, using the scroll bar next to the **Trend Lines** box, choose **Polynomial of the 3rd Degree**.

 Third-degree polynomials are algebraic expressions using numbers multiplied by themselves. For example, $X * X * X$ is represented as X^3, and a polynomial algebra expression would be represented by $y = ax^3 + bx^2 + cx + d$, where x and y are the chart axes. This particular trend line type was chosen because it provided the most information with this chart data. Experiment with the other choices and decide for yourself.

6. Click on **OK** and review your QlikView created trend line.

Experiment with the other trend line options to become familiar with the results they produce. Notice that you can select several trend line types at once. Also, notice that they are all defaulting to the same color as the measure line so that we do not have the visually distinct color option as we do with creating our own trend formula, which is what we did in the first chart.

Extending a trend line into a forecast line

Open **Properties** for **12 Month Rolling Average**, and return the current trend line display to a single line based on **Sales** using **Polynomial of the 3rd Degree**. Now we will extend that line into a forecast line:

1. Navigate to the **Axes** tab.

2. Notice that, in the lower-right corner, there are two boxes. One is labelled **Backcast** and the other is labelled **Forecast**:

Figure 6-3: Backcast and Forecast selection

3. Check each box and enter a number to represent the number of periods to extend **Forecast** and the number of periods to extend **Backcast**.

4. Before you close **Properties**, navigate to the **Fonts** tab, choose **Size 8** for the list boxes and charts, and click on **Apply** so that the time periods will be easier to distinguish.

Rather than using a built-in formula, we can base **Forecast** on a custom formula-based trend line similar to the one we used in the first chart. The chart for **12 Month Rolling Average** will now look like the following screenshot:

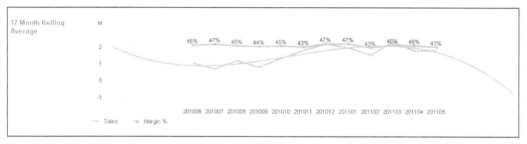

Figure 6-4: Backcast and Forecast displayed on a chart

The nuts and bolts of the trending dashboard

The **Trending** dashboard is located on the left-hand side of the **Sales Analysis** dashboard. It consists of four quadrants of bar charts that can successfully be viewed all at once; the selection section matches the other dashboards. These, in general, are good choices.

Each of the four charts has a **Drill-down group** button that allows us to get to successive dimensions and layers of detail in a particular chart. And the charts all interact with each other, providing additional information about the category we are drilling into. For example, if we choose **New Zealand** in the lower-right corner **Region Chart**, we can see in the upper-left corner **Segment Change Chart** that we have a profit margin on **Wholesale Liquor**; with both **New Zealand** and **Australia** on the grid, however, we have a loss margin. We can also see in the **Product Change Chart** directly above the **Region Chart** that **Baked Goods** are only a small contributor in **New Zealand** and that **Deli** makes the largest **Product** contribution.

Clearing Selections to bring **Australia** back on the grid now shows **Wholesale Liquor** to be a loss leader in **Australia** for the upper-left corner **Segment Change Chart**. It also looks as if **Jenny Davidson** is **Zone Manager** with the loss in **Liquor** sales in the lower-left chart displaying **Change in Margin** related to **Sales Manager/ Rep**. And it looks like **Baked Goods** seems to be a profit leader in **Product Change in Margin**; that is, until we try to drill down into the longest bar in the chart and discover that the line actually represents **Fruit**.

Confusing us further, if we select 2010, suddenly **Segment Change** flips and **Wholesale Grocery** becomes the loss leader and is in the top row, while **Wholesale Liquor** moves to the bottom row. **Jenny Davidson** had a much better year in 2010 for **Wholesale Liquor**, while **Chris Parkin** appears to have really missed his quota on **Wholesale Groceries**. And if we drill down further, we can see that **John Greg** is the salesperson who will soon be looking for a new job.

Colors

This set of charts is color-coordinated in lavender and light green. An unusual choice, perhaps it was made so that colors did not imply good or bad in the margin display. But if that was the reason, it would have been better to choose a single color since the bars extend from zero to the right-hand side or the left-hand side with positive or negative numbers respectively. These two particular hues are very poor for an executive with red-green color blindness as they would appear as almost identical shades of gray, losing any visual distinction based on color. Perhaps a blue and a yellow would have accomplished the same result without the potential display issue.

The colors used in the **Trending** dashboard are set via color formulas and then locked down so deeply that we cannot change them without destroying the layout. We will examine using a **Theme** to change colors in our QlikView document later in this chapter, but, right now, we can learn how to create a **Color Formula**.

Right-click on the upper-left quadrant chart, **Segment Change in Margin**, and choose **Properties**. Navigate to the **Colors** tab, and notice that the first color sample in the upper-left corner has a little formula symbol **f(x)**. The following figure shows this:

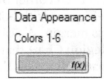

Figure 6-5: Color sample with the formula symbol

Double-click on **Color Sample** to bring up a wizard for **Color Area**. In the **Color Area** wizard, you can see that the radio button for **Calculated** is selected and a formula is entered into the box with ellipses (...). Clicking on the ellipses brings up the following formula:

```
if((If(Measure='Margin', Sum({<[Fiscal Year] = {$(vCurrentYear)},Fisca
lMonthNum = {"<=$(vCurrentMonthNum)"}>}
[Sales Margin Amount]) - Sum({<[Fiscal Year] = {$(=(vCurrentYear)
- 1)}, FiscalMonthNum = {"<=$(vCurrentMonthNum)"} > }[Sales Margin
Amount]), Sum({<[Fiscal Year] = {$(vCurrentYear)},FiscalMonthNum =
{"<=$(vCurrentMonthNum)"}>} [Sales Amount]) - Sum({<[Fiscal Year] =
{$( = (vCurrentYear)-1)}, FiscalMonthNum = {"<=$(vCurrentMonthNum)"}>}
[Sales Amount]))))>0,
RGB(102,204,102), RGB(255,0,0))
```

The very last row of the formula RGB(0,255,255),RGB(0,0,255) assigns colors to the chart bars. **RGB(102,204,102)** is pale green and **RGB(255,0,0)** is red. We cannot affect changes to the color formula on the **Trending** tab because a theme has been applied to the sheet object that protects it from having changes made. We can, however, create our own sheet to experiment with colors and learn more.

Experimenting with color formulas

To experiment with color formulas, create your own chart on your **Copy of Sales Analysis** tab or create a new tab.

1. Create your new sheet:

    1. Go to the **Layout** menu and choose **New Sheet**.
    2. After the new sheet appears, right-click to bring up the context menu and choose **Properties**.
    3. Rename your new sheet Color Test in the **Title** on the **General** tab.
    4. Click on **OK**.

2. Add your chart:

    1. Right-click on your sheet and choose the **New Sheet** object.
    2. Choose **Chart**.
    3. In the **General** tab, title your chart Sales Color Test and, for **Type**, choose **Bar Chart** (the first one).
    4. Click on **Next**.
    5. Scroll down and choose **Segment Group** for **Used Dimension**.
    6. Click on **Next**.

7. In the **Expression** wizard, type in or select and paste this formula:
   ```
   Sum ([Sales Margin Amount])
   ```

8. Click on **OK** to close the Expression wizard.

9. Label your measure **Margin**.

10. Click on **Next** and Next again to get to the **Style Wizard** page.

11. Choose the horizontal orientation instead of the vertical orientation.

12. Click on **Next** to take the defaults for **Presentation**.

13. Click on **Next** to take the defaults for **Axes**.

14. On the **Colors Wizard** page, click on the first **Data Appearance Color** block to bring up the **Color Area Wizard** page.

15. Switch the radio button to **Calculated**.

16. Click on the ellipses to bring up the **Expression** wizard page, and enter the following formula:
    ```
    If(Sum ([Sales Margin Amount])>0,RGB(0,255,255),
    RGB(0,0,255))
    ```

17. Click on **OK** to close the **Expression** wizard; the color area changes to a bright turquoise blue and shows the formula symbol.

18. Click on **Next**, **Next**, **Next**, and **Finish** or just click on **Finish** to accept defaults for the rest of the wizard.

3. Now, add a list box to see your colors change:

   1. Right-click and choose the **New Sheet Object** from the context menu.

   2. Choose **List Box**.

   3. Choose the dimension **Drill-Through Group Product Drill**.

   4. Name your **List Box** Product Drill.

   5. Click on **OK**.

4. Now, to see the effects of your formula, we have to find a negative **Sales Margin** sum. Thus, in your new **Product Drill List Box**:

   1. Choose **Deli**.

   2. Then, choose **Side Dishes**.

   3. Finally, choose **American Cole Slaw**.

Our amounts under the chart switch to negative numbers, and our bar changes to a medium-hued royal blue. Save your QlikView document under a new name or over your current document if you want to experiment on your own later:

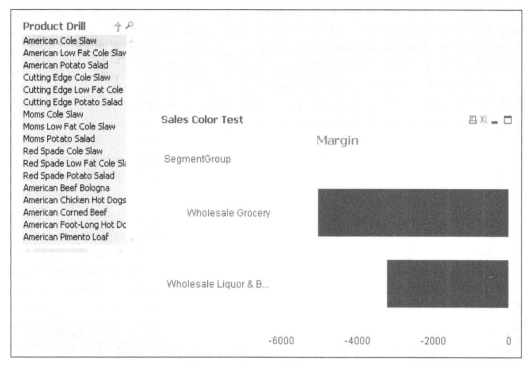

Figure 6-6: Negative Sales margin

How to get other colors

The color codes we used in our formula were actually Visual Basic Red, Blue, and Green designations. RGB(0,255,255) is yellow and RGB(0,0,255) is blue. For some undocumented reason, when they are used together in a formula for color in a horizontal bar chart, they blend together for the first color, so in **Color Test Chart**, we get bright turquoise. On the **Trending** tab, the pale green RGB(102,204,102) and the red RGB(255,0,0) blend to give us the lavender colored bars. Perhaps it works similar to the expression shortcuts where 1 allows us to go backwards and forwards, while $ in the top expression freezes. These are the color codes used in HTML to designate colors in a web page.

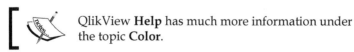 QlikView **Help** has much more information under the topic **Color**.

For additional help with color selection in the RGB Visual Basic code, please visit:

`http://www.tayloredmktg.com/rgb/` or `http://rapidtables.com/web/color/RGB_Color.htm`

Another way to get the RGB numbers is to open Microsoft Paint and click on the **Edit Colors** button to pop up the **Colors** interface. After picking a color, you can see the numbers to use for Red, Green, and Blue. Also, **Hue**, **Saturation**, and **Luminosity** will be shown and can be used to modify the numbers and therefore the colors in QlikView objects.

Layout themes

We cannot see what theme is applied by opening the **Sheet Properties** wizard, and the only way to tell what is in **Theme** is to examine the XML code. Nonetheless, themes are very useful.

The QlikView **Layout Theme** is a set of formatting properties that can be applied to a whole QlikView layout or to specific documents or charts. **Layout Theme** files are stored in the QlikView theme folder, normally found under the `Windows Application Data` folder for the active user. **Layout Theme** files are coded in XML and can be manually edited in an XML editor but are easier for most of us to manage through the **Theme Maker Wizard**.

To examine the **Theme Maker Wizard**, right-click in a vacant area of the **Trending** sheet and bring up **Sheet Properties**. On the **General** tab, you will find a **Theme Maker** button that will allow you to create a new **Theme**, and the **Apply Theme** button that will allow you to switch between the theme you created and the existing one. The **Theme Maker Wizard** is located in the **Layout** tab for the objects on a sheet because you can have themes for any level of QlikView objects. For the **Clear Selections** button on the **Sales Analysis** tab, you will find the button for **Theme Maker Wizard** located on the **Layout** tab of the **Properties Wizard**.

 You will find a large number of themes that you downloaded when you installed QlikView. You can find them by navigating to:

`C:/Program Files/QlikView/Themes`

Themes are useful in creating a consistent look throughout a QlikView document and in enforcing a company style so that all QlikView documents are branded in the company's approved colors, fonts, border, caption styles, and printer settings for printable object types. Try applying `Themes` that came with QlikView to **Sales Color Test Chart**. The following screenshot shows this themes available to apply:

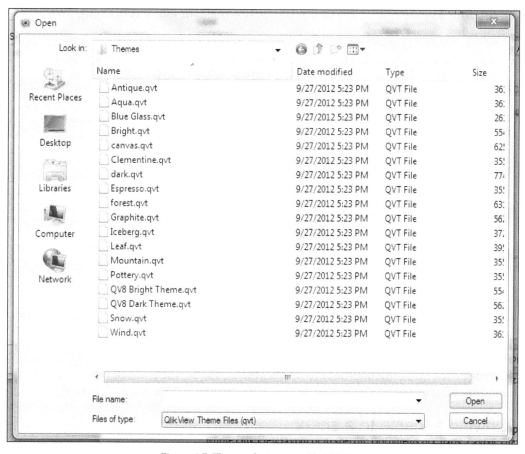

Figure 6-7: Themes that came with QlikView

Creating your own theme

As you can see in the preceding screenshot, there are multiple general-purpose Themes provided with the QlikView installation package, but, if you want to create your own theme, follow these steps:

1. Format a Qlikview document via **Properties** to your preferences.

2. Format **Sheet Properties** of one sheet to your preferences.

3. Then, create and format one sheet object of each type (**List Box**, **Chart**, **Statistics Box**, and **Button**) to your preferences. Caption/Border properties usually only need to be formatted once on one of the sheet objects.

4. Now, open the **Theme Maker Wizard** from the **Layout** tab for the sheet, and create a new theme by inserting properties from the first of the formatted objects you created (the order does not matter).

5. Run **Theme Maker Wizard** repeatedly—once for every remaining formatted object you created.

Applying your new theme

QlikView **Layout Themes** can be applied either manually, after a new QlikView Document is started, or automatically, every time a new QlikView object is created. Themes can be applied to individual sheet objects or to groups of sheet objects. Themes can also be applied to a whole sheet or an entire QlikView document.

To apply a theme to QlikView objects, follow these steps:

Applying a theme to a whole document

1. Open the document or activate it by clicking on it.
2. Open **Document Properties Wizard** from the **Settings** menu.
3. Go to the **Layout** tab.
4. Click on the **Apply Theme** button.
5. Select your theme via the browser dialog.
6. Click on **OK**.

All **Properties** in the theme that are applicable to the document will now be applied, including all sheets and sheet objects that have formats in the theme applied.

Applying a theme to a sheet

1. Activate the sheet by clicking on its tab.
2. Open the **Sheet Properties Wizard** via a right-click or from the **Settings** menu.
3. Go to the **General** tab.
4. Click on the **Apply Theme** button.
5. Select your theme via the browser dialog.
6. Click on **OK**.

The theme will be applied to all applicable objects on the selected sheet.

Applying a theme to a sheet object

1. Click on the QlikView sheet object to activate it.
2. Right-click to get the context menu, and open the **Properties Wizard** for the sheet object.

3. Navigate to the **Layout** tab.

4. Click on the **Apply Theme** button.

5. Select your theme via the browser dialog.

6. Click on **OK**.

Theme Properties that are applicable to the selected sheet object will now be applied. To apply your theme to a group of sheet objects, you must first make them all active by holding down the *Shift* key and clicking each object or by lassoing around the selected objects.

The nuts and bolts of the What If? dashboard

We will now examine the **What If?** dashboard to see what ideas it can generate for our own QlikView documents. The **What If?** tab is located on the right-hand side of the **Sales Analysis** tab. It is a reasonably simple example of an input multiplied by measures to display the results. The **Slider** changes what shows in the **Input Box**, but the **Input Box** does not always change the **Slider**, especially if the number entered is outside the slider range. The sliders look as if you can pick an interval between one and five or between five and ten but, in reality, you are limited to intervals of 5 percent. Manually, you can click in the interval display box and then click on the ellipses (…). This will pop up an **Expression Wizard** page, where you could enter an expression or just an intermediate number, such as 2.5 or -17.

We can also see that the **Selection** layout is the same as the other dashboards. Again, this consistency is a good choice.

So, how do the What If ? **Input Box** percentages work to adjust the numbers in the **Straight Table Chart** object? Right-click on the **Input Box** (the first one) where we can type a formula or enter a number. Here, we can see that it is indeed an **Input Box** object; on the **General** tab, the properties show that it creates a new variable named vVolume.

The **Slider** underneath the nicely formatted **Input Box** is a **Slider/Calendar** object using the same variable created by and for the **Input Box**; the variable is named vVolume.

Now, if we right-click, bring up the properties of **Straight Table Chart** (Object **CH50**), and navigate to the **Expressions** tab, we can see that each of the columns in the **Straight Table** has an expression. The following screenshot shows this:

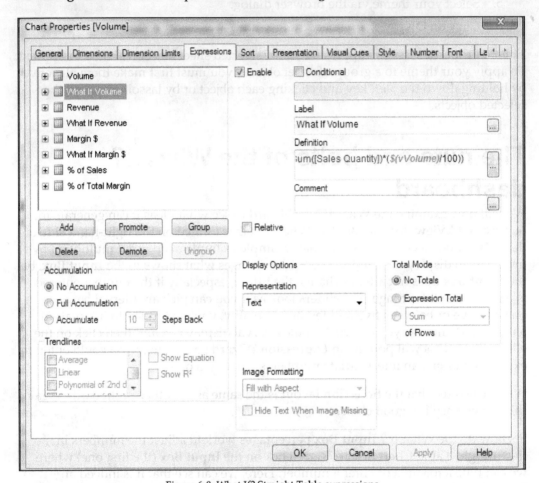

Figure 6-8: What If? Straight Table expressions

If we then click on the expression named **What if Volume**, we can see that the formula is Sum([Sales Quantity])+(Sum([Sales Quantity])*($(vVolume)/100)). It uses the same vVolume variable to multiply the Sales Quantity measure to increase the measure by the percentage entered or picked with the **Slider**. It is a pretty simple but effective way of creating what-if scenarios.

 Don't forget that a **Straight Table** can be exported to Excel after creating a scenario. Right-click on it to bring up the context menu and choose **Send to Excel**.

Summary

In this section, You learned how to create trend and forecast lines in charts using the existing **Sales Analysis** dashboard. You learned about creating color formulas to customize the color display of your objects and created a new chart to test your color formula. You learned how to create and apply a theme to all kinds of QlikView objects, from the QlikView document itself to individual fonts and borders. You learned how to create an **Input Box** with a variable and to apply that variable in a formula.

In the next chapter, we will examine the Inventory dashboard.

Summary

QlikView Inventory Analysis

7

In this chapter, we will cover the QlikView **Inventory** tab in the CFO example dashboard for ideas to use in tracking and reporting on Inventory. We will do the following things:

- Teach you more about good and bad design choices in dashboard design
- Investigate the potential KPI measure: *Inventory Turns*
- Examine the nuts and bolts of the **Inventory** tab of the CFO example dashboard

Reopening the CFO dashboard

We are going to start with the **Inventory** sheet of the Executive Dashboard.qvw from the examples we downloaded when we installed QlikView. If it is not open, open it now and navigate to the **Inventory** tab:

1. Open QlikView if it is not open already.
2. Using the **File | Open** menu in QlikView, navigate to **Program Files | QlikView | Examples | Documents** and double-click Executive Dashboard.qvw to open it.
3. Select the last tab: the **Inventory** tab.

Delving into the four-quadrant layout

Right away, we notice that not only are the controls laid out intuitively like the other tabs, but also this page has a nice four-quadrant layout that is similar to the look we created when we created our new **Sales Analysis** tab. Four-quadrant layouts are often the easiest visualization for human beings to mentally organize. Each quadrant is essentially the same size, implying that they are of equal importance in the information they provide. More than a handful of items on a single page requires too much thought to quickly prioritize. Humans who are taught to read from left to right will also tend to assume that the upper left-hand side quadrant is the most important. This dashboard is definitely organized to display the most important pieces of information on the top row, but the left-hand bar graph requires more time to register what it represents and to interpret, while the right-hand table, though not as pretty, certainly draws your eyes because you want to see the numbers arranged in meaningful ways. Once you have learned to use them together, you can find items not meeting your expectations and drill down for detail easily. Not only do you have the visual aspect, but you have the numbers associated with this at your fingertips.

The good and bad of the Inventory tab

In the left-hand side upper-horizontal bar chart that we have been looking at, we can see **Inventory Turns** in orange and the total **Value** of the stock in blue. We also have a vertical bar to establish an average inventory value that we would like to maintain. At least, we assume that is what the bar represents since it is the same color as the horizontal **Value** bar and since it has the **Target** label next to it in the same color. Unfortunately, to see all the product lines, we need to use a scrollbar. Perhaps we should either forego the bottom row to add room to display everything, or group our product lines into a few high-level groups that can then be drilled down on for detail.

For example, if I use the bar graph, I can see **Dairy**, and it stands out because it has the fewest inventory turns. That seems very curious to me as I would expect dairy products to be perishable and require more inventory turns than **Frozen Food**, the row above **Dairy**. Also **Dairy Products Group** represents 18 percent of what we can immediately see and 11 percent of our total **Inventory** value but has very low inventory turns compared to the other product lines, which are readily visible. Unfortunately, nothing on the screen tells me what percent of the inventory value **Dairy** represents. To get those comparisons, we have to scroll all the way to the bottom of the right-hand side **List Box** to get the grand total inventory value. Then, we scroll back up to get the **Dairy** value and use a calculator to do the math.

Another inconvenience is that changing the top bar selection of years and months changes the order in which items are displayed in the graph and list. This tells us immediately what the highest-value **Product** line is in a given time period, but it means that, when we go back to look at what happened with **Dairy**, it has moved. So, perhaps, although this is an interesting demonstration of what can be done, because we are dealing with so much information it is not a good example of what should be done. Three of the four quadrants use a measure labeled **Inventory Turn Over**. What does that represent?

What is inventory turnover?

The standard calculation for **Inventory Turns** is the *Cost of Goods Sold* from the *Income Statement* divided by the *Average Inventory for the Period*.

The number of days a company should be able to sell through its inventory varies greatly from industry to industry. Retail stores and grocery chains are going to have a much higher inventory turn rate since they are selling small-priced products. Companies that manufacture heavy machinery, such as trucks and construction equipment, are going to have a much lower turnover rate since each of their products may sell for hundreds of thousands of dollars.

In this case, we are looking at a grocery store or wholesale grocery, so the earlier question about **Dairy** turnover needs to start with the formula being used in QlikView. Start by right-clicking on the right-hand side list display and choosing **Properties**. Next navigate to the **Expressions** tab and place your cursor on the **Inventory Turns** expression to see the calculation in the **Definition** box. In the box, you will see the following formula:

```
Sum(ThroughputQty*CostPrice)/Sum(StockOH*CostPrice)
```

We cannot tell whether this is a valid formula for **Inventory Turns** based on the definition, but it looks as though it might be taking the number of units sold in the given period multiplied by the cost of the units to get the **Cost of Goods Sold** amount in dollars. Then, it is dividing by the remaining stock on hand multiplied by the cost of the units. Hopefully, if this was a real operation, reporting real numbers instead of just a demonstration, the appropriate average functions would take place before they reached the numbers used in this formula.

So, we can bring this formula down to a level suitable for comparison purposes if we have:

- 4,000 cartons of milk that have sold in this month at $2 each
- 4,200 cartons of milk last month, again sold at $2 each

- 1,100 cartons of milk remain at the end of this month, costing $1 each
- 800 cartons of milk remain at the end of last month, costing $1 each

We will assume there is no leftover stock from the prior month, since milk is a perishable item, for ease of calculation. We are going to have the following mathematical calculations to get to the one month **Inventory Turns** for this month: `(4000 * $1.00)/(((1100 * $1.00) +(800 * $1.00))/2 ) = 4.2`. We used 1 dollar in this example formula to make the math simple.

That gives about four inventory turns in the month. But we do not know if that is good or bad without comparing that to industry averages and prior performance. For dairy inventory turns comparison information, you will find a good article at:

`http://www.cooperativegrocer.coop/articles/2004-01-09/controlling-your-inventory`

At an individual product level and individual month, inventory turns is only a viable measure if we understand what it means in terms of our business. By setting goals for inventory turns for each category, we can evaluate specific items in stock and create fluid inventory averages to better manage product flow.

Other measures at the dashboard level

Going back to our manually calculated 11 percent of inventory value for the **Dairy Product** group, to have the percentage of inventory value readily available in our **Inventory** dashboard would be useful in understanding what the **Inventory Turns** might mean. If we have 11 percent of our cost of goods tied up in a set of items that is turning over more slowly than our other product groups, we might want to look at ways to increase turnover, particularly of a perishable item. But we may be limited by supply and demand. We have to stock the items because our customers expect availability, but there may be constraints outside our control.

Inventory on hand

The upper-right corner list box displays numbers related to the graphs and changes them when drilled into. The top column header say that the right-most column is **Inventory Turns**, but the display is in alphabetical order of the rows, so we have to scroll down to see **Dairy**. Alternatively, we can close each group to see just the top level product group by clicking on the minus sign (-) next to each group, turning it into a plus sign (+):

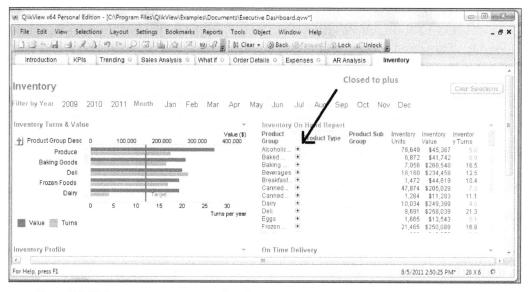

Figure 7-1: Click on any minus signs to close the Group detail and display a plus sign to make more Groups visible

Inventory profile

When looking at **Inventory Profile** in the lower-left-hand side quadrant, we can see that the majority of the value we have in products has inventory turns of less than three. Therefore, **Dairy Product Group** with **Inventory Turns** of 4.01 seems reasonable:

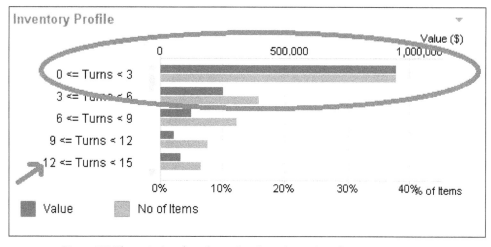

Figure 7-2: The majority of product values have fewer than three inventory turns

By clicking on the bottom turnover line for between **12** and **15** inventory turns, we bring **Breakfast Foods** and **Produce** at the top of our list on the bar chart under **Inventory Turns and Value**. Suddenly, we are presented with a totally different picture. The **Inventory Turns & Value** bar chart in the upper-left corner shows **Breakfast Foods** as having the highest **Value** and **Turns**. The **Inventory On Hand Report** shows a selection of product groups with turns in the **12** to **15** range with **Alcoholic Beverages** at the top because of the alphabetical order. Suddenly, **Dairy Group** is showing **Inventory Turns** of **14.6** percent. How can that be when it was in the **4 percent** range before?

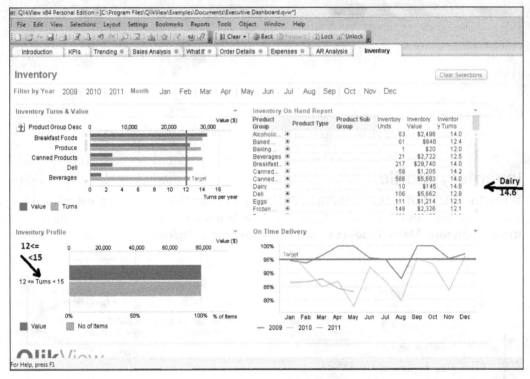

Figure 7-3: Click on any minus signs to close the Group detail and display a plus sign to make more Groups visible

We have to drill back down by opening the plus sign next to **Dairy** and rearrange our list to discover that this represents only one item within **Dairy Group — Cheese**.

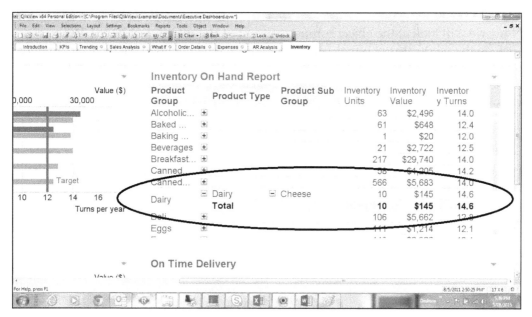

Figure 7-4: Drill down into Dairy to reveal a high turnover inventory item in cheese

On time delivery

The lower right-hand side quadrant has a line chart of **On Time Delivery**. We can see that we have a **Target** of 95 percent on-time delivery. We can also see that the lines compare our on-time delivery year over year just as in the common size income statement we built in *Chapter 2, QlikView Dashboard Financial KPIs* — another good use for year-over-year line graphs.

Here, we can see that we did better in 2009 than in 2010 or in the current year. We are building 2011. Looking closer, we can also see that the scale is 85 percent to 100 percent, so we are not doing quite as badly as we would be if that was a range of 50 percent on-time to 100 percent on-time, but we are still failing to meet our goals quite often. Our formula for our delivery on-time measure is:

```
Sum([Late Shipment])/Count([OrderID])
```

One of the questions that we might ask is whether **Target** is set realistically. Since we do not know what constitutes the **Late Shipment** measure or whether the **Target** is 10 minutes, 10 hours, or 10 days, all this really tells us is that we want more information to see whether improvement is needed in our delivery schedule or an adjustment of our **Target**.

The nuts and bolts of the Inventory dashboard

Now, we will look at the object components of the **Inventory** dashboard. When we click on the white area of our sheet object, we can see that again we have a container object, but this container only contains text and lines and two list boxes, one for the fiscal year and one for the fiscal month. What about the charts? Also, what is that looking like a complicated list box in the right-hand side quadrant?

The pivot table

When we open the properties of the object in the upper-right-hand side corner, the **Inventory On Hand Report**, we can see that the object is actually a **Pivot Table**. We have not worked with a **Pivot Table** object before:

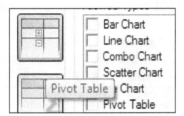

Figure 7-5: Closeup of the Pivot Table icon on the General tab

Since this is the first time that we have worked with a **Pivot Table**, open **Properties** by right-clicking and choosing **Properties** in the context menu so that we can see what is unique about a **Pivot Table** object.

On the **Dimensions** tab, we can see that we are using three **Dimensions**:

- Product Group Desc
- Product Type Desc
- Product Sub Group Desc

These correspond to the three columns of text data in the **Pivot Table**:

On the **Expression** tab, we have three expressions that correspond with the three columns of numbers in the **Inventory On Hand Report Pivot Table**:

- Inventory Units
- Inventory Value
- Inventory Turns

On the **Sort** tab, we notice that **Product Group**, the first on the list, is set to sort by **STATE** ascending and then **Text A-> Z**, which means **Product Group** will first sort at that level by the first measure value and then alphabetically.

The next one is the **Presentation** tab. There are settings on the **Presentation** tab that we need to pay attention to in order to understand what the **Pivot Table** is doing. When we have **Product Group** highlighted, we can see that we also have the following status:

- The checkbox for **Partial Sum** is checked – this tells the **Pivot Table** to display our measures when subgroups are included.

- The checkbox for **Allow Pivoting** is checked – this option must be selected to allow the usual pivoting function of a pivot table.

- Use the checkbox for **Vertical Text on Column Labels** to rotate the column header to a vertical orientation. In this case, it is not checked.

- The checkbox for **Selection Indicators** is checked, and this causes a colored indicator to display in the header of any field dimension where a selection has been made – a small green-filled circle. This is shown in the following figure:

Figure 7-6: The small green-filled dot next to the selected dimensions

- The checkbox for **Always Fully Expanded** disallows the collapse of dimensions by clicking on the minus icons and is not used in this **Pivot Table**.

- The checkbox for **Suppress Expansion Icons in Print** suppresses the plus icon (+) and minus (-) icon for expand and collapse visibility when printing the sheet object. It is not selected in this **Pivot Table**.

- The checkbox for **Suppress Zero-Values** eliminates columns or rows that contain only zeros from the table display. We are using zero suppression for our display.

- The checkbox for **Suppress Missing** eliminates columns or rows that are empty from the table display. They are visible but grayed out and will not let us change the setting.

- The checkbox for **Populate Missing Cells** maps cells in cross tables representing missing combinations of dimensions to a regular null value, allowing us to use expression testing for null. This is in use in this **Pivot Table**.

- The **Null Symbol** and **Missing Symbol** text boxes allow us to enter the preferred display symbol for null and missing data.

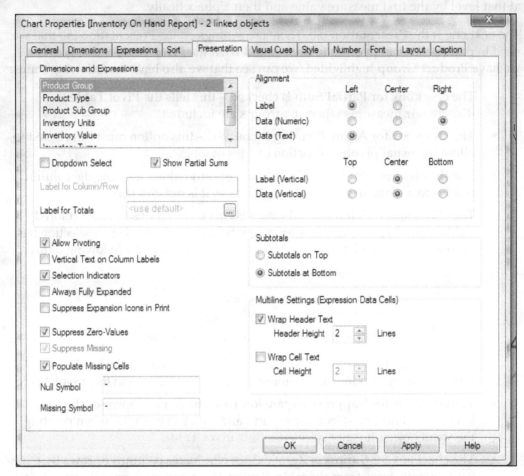

Figure 7-7: Presentation tab of the Pivot Table Properties wizard

On the right-hand side, the **Subtotals** group of radio buttons is used to set the display of totals and subtotals in the **Inventory On Hand Report Pivot Table**. The **Multiline Settings** section tells the **Pivot Table** whether or not to wrap text within the groupings.

Creating the inventory profile ranges

On the lower-left-hand side quadrant, we have the **Inventory Profile Chart**. Its colors are consistent with the other charts on the sheet. Therefore, at first glance, we would think that the orange bars would be **Inventory Turns**, but they actually represent a count of items. Now, we will examine how this range is created for the two measures represented by the orange-colored and the blue-colored bars.

When we right-click and choose **Properties** for the **Inventory Profile Chart**, we see that our dimension is **Class Turns**. If we close **Properties**, right-click on the white space to bring up the context menu, and choose **New Sheet Object** and the object type of **List Box**. With the selection of **Class Turns**, we can see that the **Class Turns** dimension already has the ranges built-in the following screenshot:

Class Turns
0 <= Turns < 3
3 <= Turns < 6
6 <= Turns < 9
9 <= Turns < 12
12 <= Turns < 15
15 <= Turns < 18
18 <= Turns < 21
21 <= Turns < 24
24 <= Turns < 27
27 <= Turns < 30
30 <= Turns < 33
33 <= Turns < 36
36 <= Turns < 39
42 <= Turns < 45
45 <= Turns < 48
48 <= Turns < 51
51 <= Turns < 54
57 <= Turns < 60

Figure 7-8: List Box of Class Turns members

There is not much to learn about the **Class Turns** dimension except that we can create our own lists and then turn around and use them in dimensions. Actually, the only item of interest that shows us something new under **Inventory Profile Properties** is the formula for *Number of Items* found on the **Expressions** tab. The formula is:

```
Count(Distinct [Item-Branch Key])
```

This is interesting because it shows us how to create a Count Distinct formula to get the count of unique items in a set.

Summary

In this section, we examined another four-quadrant dashboard layout and whether the choices on this one were appropriate to convey information about **Inventory**. You learned about calculating the KPI, **Inventory Turns**. We examined the **Properties** of a **Pivot Table** and how it differs from a list box. We were reminded that we can create our own lists, load them, and use them in dimensions. We also examined a formula for getting the count of unique items in a set.

In the next chapter, we will examine the **Order Details** dashboard.

8

QlikView Order Details Dashboard

In this chapter, we will study the **Order Details** tab in the CFO dashboard and the **Order and Inventory Management** online QlikView demo for ideas to use in supply chain analysis. The topics that we will cover are as follows:

- Analysis of the usefulness of the **Order Details** tab
- The online **Order and Inventory Management** QlikView demo
- The nuts and bolts of the **Order Details** tab

Reopening the CFO dashboard

We are going to work with the **Order Details** sheet of the Executive Dashboard. qvw from the examples that we downloaded when we installed QlikView. Open QlikView if it is not open already.

1. Using the **File | Open** menu in QlikView, navigate to the **Program Files | QlikView | Examples | Documents** folder and double-click to open Executive Dashboard.qvw.

2. Select the sixth tab: **Order Details**.

Analyzing the order details dashboard display

The **Order Details** dashboard opens and responds quickly when we click on the items in the large, straight table in the sheet. The display does this because the data is not dependent upon calculations, but is preloaded detail data that is just summed up. This is one of the great advantages of QlikView as an analysis medium: its ability to quickly load, sum up, and display large amounts of data in a concise fashion.

The rest of the display on the sheet consists of the **Multi Box**, which is used to select members from the various groups within the linked straight table, and the two small summary straight tables on the left-hand side of the sheet. The **Multi Box**, as usual, hides the **Country**, but we already know that there are only **Australia** and **New Zealand** as choices anyway.

One of the things that we immediately notice is that there seems to be a lot of negative revenue highlighted in red. If we pick **Watcom International**, one of the customers associated with the red **Sales** numbers, and we spread out the **Order Date** column, we can see some strange-looking dates. The load has the **Order Date** in the day/month/year order. A strange choice, but it does sort in the date order when we select a month in the filters. When we don't have a month selected in the filter, the data sorts alphabetically, by customer. There is no format code to switch the display to a more familiar way. However, to make this more user friendly, we can make sure that our dates are in a sort format such as century/year/ month/day when we load our data. Otherwise, we will have to hunt for usable date ranges. If the date was displayed as 2009/05/06, we would know that 6/05/2009 is May 6, 2009. It is only when we get to displays such as 28/05/2009 that we are able to figure out that the **Order Date** is actually May 28, 2009. This also eliminates the country/language differences in the date display/interpretation.

If we clear our selections and choose **Wholesale Grocery** in our **Segment** group, 2011 as the Year, **Jenny Davidson** under **Sales Manager**, and **Pannega** as our **Customer**, both the **Sales Person** and the **Segment Desc** are automatically selected for us. We can see that **Pannega** is in the **Convenience Store Segment** and the **Sales Rep** is **Kim Williams**. If we clear out the selections again, select just the **Sales Rep** as **Kim Williams**, and then limit the year to 2011 again, we can see that **Kim Williams** is the only **Sales Rep** for **Pannega**. We can also see that Pannega, with a negative revenue of **-$2,616.57**, was not doing well at all in 2011. Additionally, there were no liquor sales to offset this return loss on the grocery items.

Switching to 2010, we can see over seventy thousand in positive sales to **Pannega**. Moreover, since only **Kim Williams** sells to **Pannega**, some of the implications that we might consider are as follows:

- Has **Pannega** found other sources for the products that we supply?

- Was **Pannega** going out of business in 2011?

- Where do we reassign **Kim Williams** if we are keeping that sales representative?

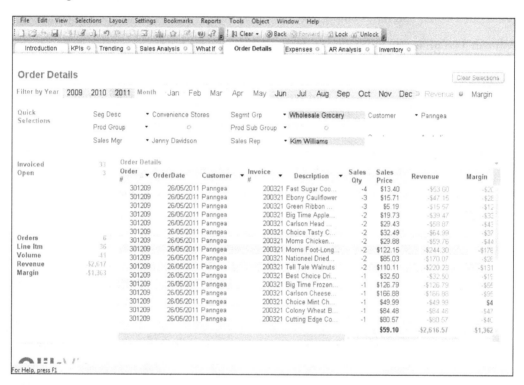

Figure 8-1: Order Details for Kim Williams in 2011

To the left in the preceding screenshot, we can see a quick summary of details such as the number of **Orders**, number of **Line Items**, **Volume**, **Revenue**, and **Margin** summarized and matching the totals at the bottom in the large straight table to the right.

Comparing the order and inventory management online demonstration

To get an idea about the other options for displaying the same types of data, a demonstration titled **Order** and **Inventory Management** is available on the QlikView website, at the following URL:

```
http://us-b.demo.qlik.com/QvAJAXZfc/opendoc.
htm?document=qvdocs%2FOrder%20and%20Inventory%20Management.
qvw&host=demo11&anonymous=true
```

You can also go to the QlikView website and search for **Order and Inventory Management**. Open the demonstration in your web browser when you find it. The first sheet with the **Dashboard** tab is more colorful and more meaningful than the *On Time Delivery line* graph that we investigated in the lower-right quadrant of the **Inventory** tab in the previous chapter. The information in the labels is more informative as well.

You may examine the **Inventory Detail** and the **What If?** tabs in this QlikView document to see if you prefer the layout choices made by the designer; but we will be reviewing the **Order Details** tab here to compare it with the one in the CFO dashboard.

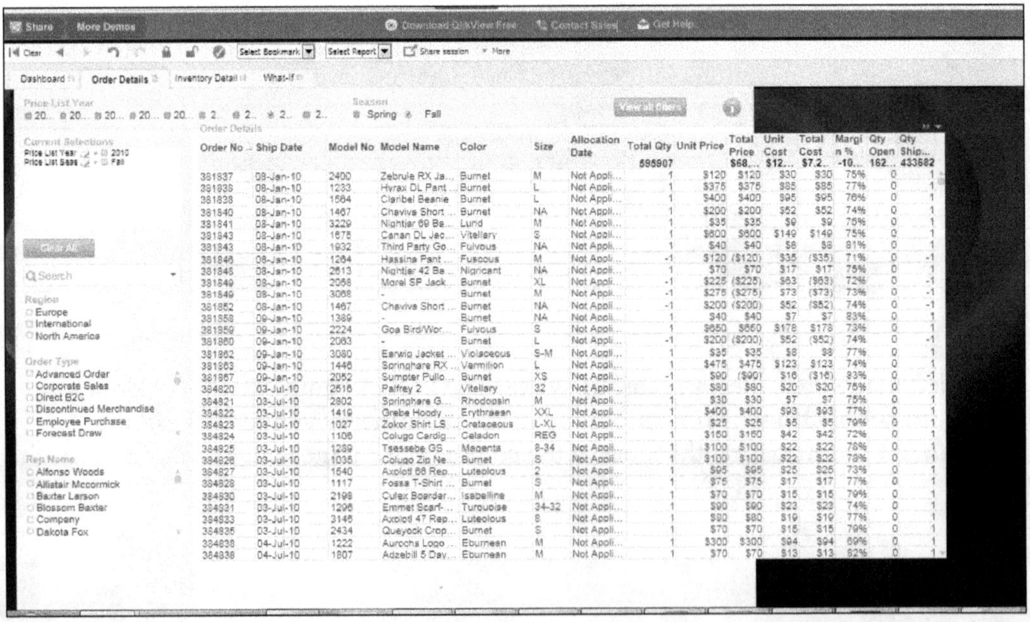

Figure 8-2: Order Details tab in Order and Inventory Management in the online demonstration

Although this dashboard is not as colorful, the absence of red may or may not be a good thing. That is because, although we are not displaying a lot of negative sales, there are some, and they don't stand out for those of us who are not red-green color blind. The red number display for the negative numbers definitely stands apart from the accounting (parentheses) used in the online demonstration.

Notice too that the date display choice in this example is more human-friendly. By hovering the mouse indicator on the right edge until we get the double-ended arrow symbol, we can pull on the right-hand side of the display. We can pull the straight table wide enough so that we can see all the data. Moreover, we do not have to use the scroll bar at the bottom of the numbers columns. It is also useful to have the **Quantity Open** and **Quantity Shipped** columns. I also prefer the clearly-labelled **Current Selections** box in the upper-left corner of the display.

Although we cannot look at the **Properties** of this **Order Details** table on the web, we can right-click and switch back and forth from a straight table to a **Pivot Table**.

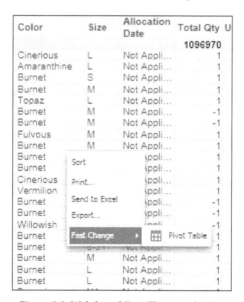

Figure 8-3: Web-based Fast Change selection

In the next section, we will learn how to change the **Order Details** tab in our CFO dashboard to allow switching between the display types, how to color-code our data and format our numbers, how to **Export a Pivot Table to Excel** for further analysis, and how to use dynamic expressions.

The nuts and bolts of the CFO dashboard order detail tab

First, since we have just discovered it is possible, we will set up a **Fast Change** type for our **Order Details** straight table. Go back to the **Order Details** tab of the CFO dashboard. Start by right-clicking on the large straight table and choosing **Properties**. In the **Properties** wizard, navigate to the first tab, **General**. Here, in the bottom right-hand side, we can see the **Fast Change** group of controls. Choose **Line Chart**, **Pivot Table**, and **Straight Table** for the **Allowed Types**.

 Be sure to choose **Straight Table** so that we can get back to where we started.

Now check the radio button in the section for **Preferred Icon Position** below the **Allowed Types** and next to **In Chart** instead of **In Caption;** click **Apply** and close the **Properties Wizard**. There will now be a small icon in the upper corner of the straight table that looks like a tiny line graph. If you click on it, the straight table changes to a pretty, but not necessarily informative, line graph, and the icon for the pivot table appears to the left of the new line graph.

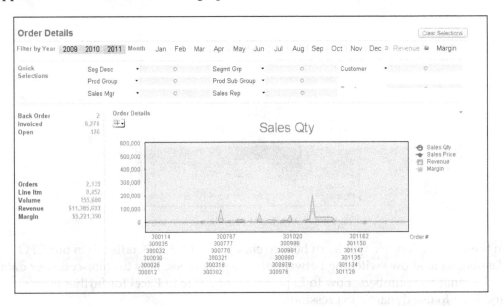

Figure 8-4: Line graph with Pivot Table Fast Change icon on the left, beneath the title

Continue by clicking the icon to the left of the line graph to switch to the pivot table; when you are done reviewing that, click the icon on the right to return to the straight table display. Now cycle through again to the pivot table.

Export to Excel

Right-click to bring up the context menu, and move down the list. You will see a couple of options near the bottom that you may not have paid much attention to before. With these options, you can **Send to Excel…** or **Export…** the data. If you cycle through the **Fast Change** to the **Line Graph**, you will get a slightly different choice: **Send Values to Excel…** in the context menu. If you want the line graph to be sent to Excel, you will need to choose **Export**. You will then export it as an image file and insert it into Excel, Word, PowerPoint, or other programs. You can also use the next option down, **Copy to clipboard**, and then paste the image. If you choose to **Export the Values**, or, from one of the other **Fast Change** screens, to **Export to Excel**, you get formatted data from the selections made at the time. Unfortunately, with the line graph on Sheet, QlikView sends the wrong column names to describe the data to Excel. You should be in the straight table to use **Export to Excel** in order to send the data to someone who does not have QlikView.

Color-coding data

How do we tell QlikView to format our negative numbers in red so that they stand out, and how do we format accounting style numbers with parentheses? Right-click in the straight table again to bring up the **Properties Wizard**. At this point, if you want to, you can turn off the **Fast Change** function by unchecking the boxes under **Fast Change** in the **General** Tab. Next, navigate to the **Visual Cues** tab. Now click on either **Sales Price**, **Revenue,** or **Margin** in the **Expressions Box** and look down at the upper and lower boxes. You will see that the lower box has a zero in it telling Qlikview that the default is red if that value is less than or equal to zero. Now change the **Normal** text to a deep blue by clicking on the black rectangle to the right in the same row as the word **Normal**. Bring up the **Color Wizard**, choose your new blue color, and click **OK**. Make sure your new color shows in the box opposite **Normal**, and close **Properties** to view your changes.

Number format patterns

To format our negative numbers, we use the **Properties Wizard** again. You may already be familiar with formatting numbers in Excel. If you are, this will be useful because QlikView, for the most part, uses the same format codes. On the **Numbers** tab in the **Properties Wizard**, you will see that the format for **Revenue** is currently given as follows:

```
$#,##0.00;-$#,##0.00
```

Change that to: `$#,##0.00;($#,##0.00)` in order to switch to an accounting format with parentheses.

Dynamic expressions

Dynamically calculated expressions can be entered almost anywhere where you can enter text such as chart titles or headings. The time required for a dynamically calculated expression to evaluate and to display is dependent on its environment and the type of data that it is required to display. For example, **dynamic expressions** in charts and tables that are defined in the expressions dialog are only calculated when the sheet object is visible and when the data changes. Dynamic expressions are not calculated when the object is minimized.

On the other hand, if the sheet object title is dynamic, this expression is evaluated each time a change occurs. Some expressions are more resource-intensive than others, and become more so with an increase in the frequency of their evaluation. The time functions, Now() and Today(), will be evaluated whenever a recalculation is required. The Now() function can especially slow down the response from the rest of the application, because it causes a recalculation of the application every second.

We can test this by creating a text box in our **Order Details** tab. Right-click in the white area of the sheet to bring up the context menu, and choose **New Sheet Object | Text Object**.

Enter the following expression in the Text Object:

```
=If (Now(),second(NOW()) , 'RED')
```

Click **OK** to display the seconds counting through the text object. The word **RED** in the expression is a placeholder and will never be displayed.

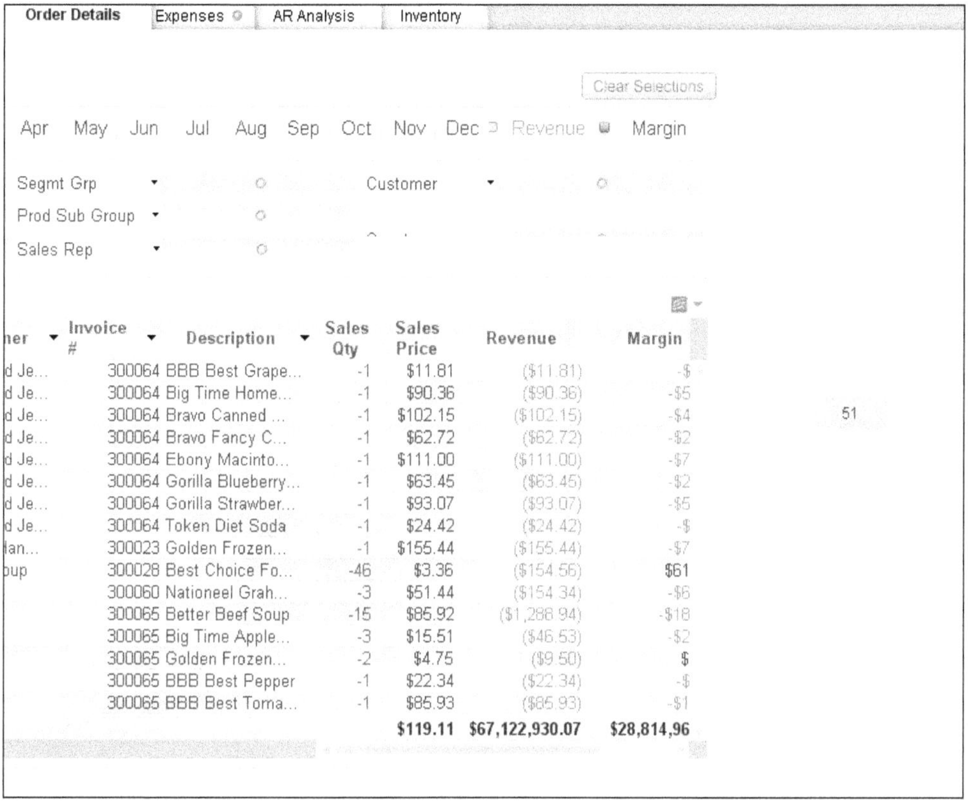

Figure 8-5: New format for negative sales and a text object counting down the seconds with the Now() function

Summary

In this chapter, we learned how to add the **Fast Change** icon to an existing sheet object. We also learned about creating data range colors to highlight information such as sales or orders below our target threshold. We discovered number format patterns to display numbers in the way we want them to be displayed. And finally, we learned how to create dynamic expressions and why they are used sparingly.

In the next chapter, we will examine the **Expenses** dashboard.

Summary

9
QlikView Expenses Dashboard

Companies often track their expenses/costs at the expense of other types of financial analysis. They do this, in part, because they have greater control over the circumstances of money outflow. Hopefully, the previous chapters have stimulated ideas for other types of information management that can be enhanced with the use of QlikView. That is why this chapter is near the end of the book.

In this chapter, we will cover the **Expenses** tab in the CFO example dashboard for ideas to use in expense reporting and management. The topics that will be covered here are as follows:

- Analysis of the usefulness of the **Expenses** tab
- The nuts and bolts of the **Expenses** tab

Reopening the CFO example dashboard

We are going to work with the **Expenses** sheet in the `Executive Dashboard.qvw` from the examples that we downloaded when we installed QlikView.
Open QlikView if it is not open already.

1. Using the **File | Open** menu in QlikView, navigate to the **Program Files | QlikView | Examples | Documents** folder and double-click the `Executive Dashboard.qvw` to open it.
2. Select the seventh tab: **Expenses**.

Analysis of the expenses dashboard display

The **Expenses** dashboard is another four-quadrant dashboard with a **Pivot Table** on the upper right-hand side, surrounded by three graphs analyzing essentially the same data in different formats. The pivot table is organized by the **Cost Center** group and reports in thousands, as the title clearly states. It is well-organized with fairly standard income-expense statement section type columns. Therefore, we can see the **2011** expenses as compared to the budget and the previous year, with the variance in both dollars and percentages. The unfavorable variances are the positive numbers shown in red; those columns must be formatted in **Properties** so that the text for those numbers is set to red when the value is greater than zero. This is just the opposite of the setting used in the previous chapter covering the **Order Details** tab. My preference would be to only have the pivot table and to have more detailed information loaded so that we can drill-down on the expense detail to a much greater level than just the general accounting line.

The pie chart in the lower left-hand corner is tied to the line chart on its immediate right. You will have to decide for yourself if the screen real estate used by the pie chart is valuable to you. The sheet objects are linked but, once we go down below the initial level of the pie chart, the line graph no longer displays data. The **General Costs** break into so many wedges that the key for the pie chart (with the percentage displayed next to it) is more useful informationally than the chart itself. If we had a greater level of detail loaded, the pie chart could become useful as a navigational device to get to the **Cost Center** and **Account** line that we might want to drill-down on.

When we examine the bar chart in the upper left-hand quadrant of the sheet, and begin clicking through the fiscal years in the selection list box, we can see that the deeper royal blue is associated with the year selected. The light turquoise blue bars are associated with the previous year. And when we get to the year 2011, the orange **Budget** line appears.

It is difficult to tell what the blue and orange lines in the line chart on the lower right-hand side represent, because we have used the same colors in all the three graphics. Are all the orange colors related? Does the royal blue represent the same thing in every graph? In this particular case, the answer is no. In the upper left graphic on the upper-left side, the royal blue is the current year, and orange represents the budget. In the pie chart, the royal blue represents the highest percentage, and the orange is used for the third-highest percentage. In the lower-right side, we are not even sure what the two lines represent since the only label is, **2010 Expen… Trend**. We can see the percentages on the left and the months across the bottom. We can also see the lines change when we change the years with **Filter by Year**, but we cannot tell which one of the lines is the **Expense** percentage and which one of the line represents the trend.

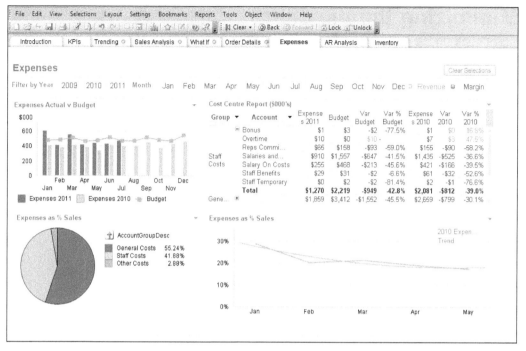

Figure 9-1: Expenses tab from CFO example dashboard

In the next section, we will investigate what the lines in the **Expenses as % Sales** line chart represent and whether our assumption about the text formatting for the pivot table is true, along with other formatting features. We will also reformat our line graph to provide easier understanding. We will set the pie chart such that it can be minimized or maximized, and we will create a link in our pivot table.

The nuts and bolts of the CFO dashboard expenses tab

First we are going to get the pie chart out of our way without deleting the object from the sheet.

Minimizing the pie chart

Right-click on the pie chart and bring up its **Properties**. Navigate to the **Caption** tab on the right. You may need to use the left < > right arrows to see it.

Figure 9-2: Caption tab: Allow Minimize and Allow Maximize checkboxes

Under the **Caption** tab, you will see the **Allow Minimize** and **Allow Maximize** checkboxes on the bottom-right corner. Check them both, click **Apply,** and close the wizard. Now you will see the standard computer display symbols for minimizing a window.

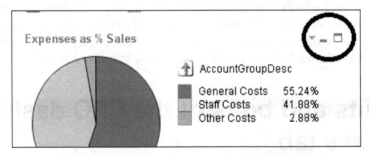

Figure 9-3: Minimize and maximize symbols now appear

Click the - symbol to minimize the pie chart and make room to spread out the line chart. Click on the words in the minimized box, and the pie chart will maximize. From the maximized chart, you can choose the - symbol again to minimize. You can also use the double-boxes symbol to restore the pie chart to its original position.

Improving the line chart

Next, we will work on the **Properties** of the line chart so we can find out what it represents and how we can improve its display. Right-click on the, **Expense as % Sales** line chart, choose **Properties,** and navigate to the **Layout** tab. Check the checkbox to **Allow Move\Size** so that we can make the image wider and see the whole label. Next, move to the **Expressions** tab. We can see that the expression is labelled **2010 Expenses** but the actual formula is as follows:

```
Sum({<[Fiscal
Year]={$(vCurrentYear)}>}ExpenseActual)/Sum({<[Fiscal
Year]={$(vCurrentYear)}>}[Sales Amount])
```

In the preceding formula, the expenses for the currently selected **Fiscal Year** are being divided by the sales amount of the currently selected **Fiscal Year.** How are we getting two lines from one expression? It is also set to calculate a trend line as a polynomial of the second degree. So, the orange line is our actual **Expenses as a % of Sales**, and the turquoise blue line is the trend line.

Now, in the same tab, click on the actual label, **2010 Expenses**, and use the ellipse button (**...**) to the right to bring up the label properties. Click on the **Functions** tab in the label properties. Here you will see that the label actually has a function attached to it:

```
dual Above ([TOTAL] expr [, offset=1[, count=1]])
```

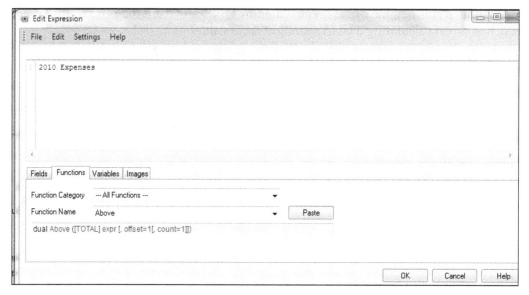

Figure 9-4: Function in the Edit Expression wizard

What does that do? Actually, this function is created automatically and is commonly used throughout the CFO example dashboard in chart objects; we have just not looked at it before. The expression dual (s , x) forces the string s (in this formula, s represents Above ([TOTAL] expr) to be associated with a number represented by the x in the expression (in this expression it is the count of 1).

> In QlikView, when several data items are read into a field with different string representations but the same number representation, they will all share the first string representation that is encountered.

This expression can be leveraged in both scripts and chart expressions. This is often used with dates so that December 2009, December 2010, and December 2012 will be displayed as **DEC**. The dual function will be used early in a given load script or expression, before the other data is loaded, so that the first string (such as DEC in this example) will be shown in the list box using the dual function.

Another QlikView expression function that can be used is Expr. It evaluates, in the expression where it is used to the value to look for in the specific field or cell of the loaded table data. So, in the expression associated with our **Expression** field, Expr evaluates to whatever is located at the offset of one.

Changing the given expression to above([total] expr [, offset [,n]]) tells QlikView to return the value of the expression from the row above the current row within a column; the offset is calculated by QlikView from the preceding function when calculating a chart's straight table value.

> The first row of a column will return a NULL value because there are no rows above the first row of a table.

If the chart is one-dimensional, or if the expression is preceded by the [Total] command, then the current value is always going to be equal to the aggregate of the entire column.

Now that we've understood that the function is telling the chart to use the totals of the expression for each intersection of the month, close **Properties** and stretch out the chart so that we can read the entire key.

Suppose we want to change the key so that it is color-coded to match the line colors that were chosen. For this, perform the following steps:

1. Right-click to bring up the line chart **Properties** again.
2. Navigate to the **Expression** tab.
3. In the middle column, second from the bottom, you will find a checkbox for putting **Text** on the axis.
4. Click on the checkbox to insert the percentages in the chart above the months.
5. Next, navigate to the **Presentation** tab. On the bottom-right side is the **Text in Chart** box.
6. Click on the lower text first, the one that says **2010 Expenses**.
7. Click **Edit**. Change the text to read **Expenses % Sales**.
8. Change the background color to orange.
9. Click **OK** to return to the **Presentation** tab.
10. Click on the word **Trend** to highlight it and activate the **Edit** button again.
11. Edit the background of the word **Trend** to a turquoise blue.
12. Click **OK** to return to the **Presentation** tab.
13. Click **Apply** to apply your changes and exit the **Properties** wizard.

Review your changes. They should look similar to what is shown in the following screenshot:

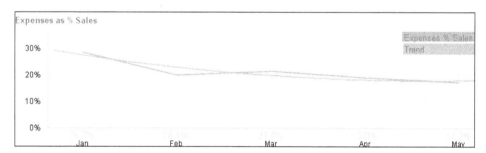

Figure 9-5: Changed line chart with the key color-coded

Now we will examine the bar chart on the upper-left side of the sheet.

Bar chart formulas

Most of what we will discuss in this section will be a review of the earlier chapters. For example, the first expression **Label** formula is =`'Expenses '&$(vCurrentYear)`, which tells QlikView to show the actual year selected, with the word **Expenses** preceding it. The actual expression formula for the first Expression is:

```
Sum({<[Fiscal Year]={$(vCurrentYear)}>}ExpenseActual)/1000
```

This tells QlikView to display the sum of the **ExpenseActual** data field divided by one thousand. The result is displayed in thousands, as indicated by the chart label **$000**.

The second formula **Label** is `'Expenses '&$(=(vCurrentYear)-1)`, which tells QlikView to get the previous year and display that with the word **Expenses** preceding it. The actual expression formula for the second expression is as follows:

```
Sum({<[Fiscal Year]={$(=(vCurrentYear)-1)}>}ExpenseActual)/1000
```

This tells QlikView to get the previous year and to display the sum of the **ExpenseActual** data field divided by one thousand. We have reviewed both of these formula patterns before.

The third and final Expression just uses the **Budget** data and the formula `Sum(ExpenseBudget)/1000`. The squares on the **Budget** line are produced by using the **Display Options** section of the **Expressions** tab.

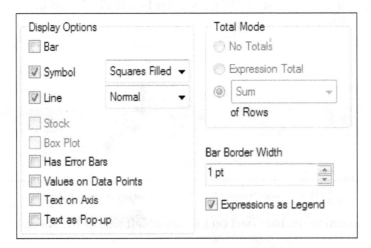

Figure 9-6: Display options used to set budget line

The **Symbol** checkbox, is checked and the option **Squares Filled** is selected. The **Line** checkbox is checked to instruct QlikView to use a line instead of a third color bar. The **Expressions as Legend** checkbox is also checked, instructing QlikView to put the legend key across the bottom with the **Label** names of the expressions.

Pivot table variances

The pivot table variances are calculated in the expressions with those labels; as we surmised, the text is color-coded by using the **Visual Cues** tab of the **Properties**. Open the **Pivot Table Properties** to examine the **Expressions** tab. Interestingly, rather than calculating just on the basis of other fields, some of the calculations use the column designation (similar to the Excel expression *A1-B1)*, and carry it down the column. For example, `Budget Var` is the expression `column(1) - Budget`, and `Budget Var %` is the expression `column(3)/column(2)`.

Formatting and linking

Next, navigate to the **Style** tab. In the upper left-hand corner, you will see the **Current Style** selection. The drop-down shows thirteen different styles to choose from. Pick a new one, and choose **Apply** to see your style changes.

If we don't have drill-down details loaded to our QlikView document, perhaps we could put in a link that would take us to an intra-company website with the additional details on the expenses that we want. We can link **Field Values** to **Links** by creating a **Link Expression** in the **Definition** field of an **Expression**. The **Definition** of the **Expression** needs to be in the following format:

`Text_to_display&<url>Text_of_url_link.`

`Text_to_Display` will be displayed in the table cell. `Text_of_url_link` will be the actual URL link that is opened in a new browser window. To create a clickable link in our Pivot Table, follow these steps:

1. Open the **Properties** of the pivot table and navigate to the **Expressions** tab.

2. Add a new expression by clicking the **Add** button; name it `MyLink`.

3. Now click in the **Definition** box of our new expression, and then click the ellipse (**...**) to bring up the **Edit Expression** window.

4. Type the following into the **Edit Expression** window: `MyLink & '<url>www.qliktech.com'`.

5. Now click **Apply**, and exit **Properties.**

Now the column named **MyLink** shows at the end of the pivot table. Under the header, the URL command and its path are displayed. Click on one of the **Link** fields; QlikView will ask you if you want to open the link.

Links can be web pages from your internal website or the World Wide Web. They can be local files from your personal computer or files located on a company-shared folder, images, or even sounds files. (For example, I really wanted to add the sound of a cow mooing to *Chapter 7, QlikView Inventory Analysis* when we were investigating the **Dairy Product Group**.)

You can create separate load files in Excel describing which information files are to be linked to each field value, and then you can tell QlikView to treat the tables created from the load files as information tables. Set up information tables with two columns. The first column should be **Field Name** and contain a list of values associated with that field. The second column can be titled with a name of your choice; it will contain the information itself or references to non-text files such as pictures or applications (such as Word and Excel).

If we load images as links, they will open in a separate viewer. But we might just like to add some custom images to a QlikView document. To see how you can do this, reopen your first QlikView document, CheyeneCo.qvw, used in *Chapter 1, Getting That Financial Data into QlikView*. You can practice by adding your own images to your document.

 There are two image files available for download from your account at http://www.PacktPub.com that can be used for this exercise. They are named Fish.jpg and Gecko.jpg.

Perform the following steps to add images to the **Main** tab:

1. Download the images from your Packt account and save them to a folder on your computer, or create some small images of your own.

2. Create an Excel file to tell QlikView about the images.

    ° The first column is labeled **Field Name** and the second column in the picture is labeled **Month Image**

    ° Input MONTH in the first column, second row

    ° Input the path to the image that you want to use from your computer (that is, C:\pictures\Fish.JPG) in the second column, second row

    ° Enter YEAR in the third row, first column

    ° Enter the path to the second image that you want to use from your computer (that is, C:\pictures\Gecko.JPG) in the second column, third row

    ° Save the Excel file at a place where you can find it via the path

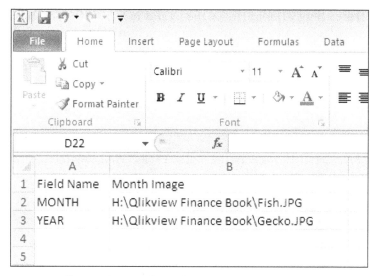

Figure 9-7: Example Excel spreadsheet for image load

3. Now, from the **Main** tab of the QlikView document, choose **Edit Script** under **File**.

4. This time, choose the **Field Data** button.

5. Choose the **Local File** radio button, and then **Browse** for the Excel file that you have created.

6. Choose **NEXT**.

7. On the **Options** tab, change the **Label** dropdown from **none** to **Embedded Labels**.

8. Choose **NEXT**.

9. Review the **File Type** tab, then click **NEXT**.

10. The new portion of the script should now look similar to the following:

```
LOAD [Field Name],
     [Month Image]
FROM
[C:\Users\User\Documents\My Docs\Packt Publishing\QlikView Finance
Book\MonthImages.xls]
(biff, embedded labels, table is Sheet1$);
```

If we were going to create links, we would now edit the script and put the word INFO before the word load in this section of the script. But we want to embed the images instead, so we are going to edit the script and put the word Bundle ahead of the word load in this section of the script. Edit your script so that this section looks similar to the following:

```
Bundle LOAD [Field Name],
      [Month Image]
FROM
[C:\Users\User\Documents\My Docs\Packt Publishing\QlikView Finance
Book\MonthImages.xls]
(biff, embedded labels, table is Sheet1$);
```

11. Now click the **OK** button to save your script.

12. From the **File** menu, **Reload** your script.

13. Next on the **Main** tab, open the **Properties** of the **Month** list box, and navigate to the **Expressions** tab.

14. Add a new expression by clicking the **Add** button.

15. Now click in the **Definition** box of the new expression, and then click the ellipse (**...**) to bring up the **Edit Expression** window.

16. Navigate to the **Images** tab of the **Edit Expression** window.

17. From the **Image Folder** dropdown, choose **Field Name/**.

18. From the **Image** dropdown, choose **MONTH**.

Figure 9-8: The Edit Expression Image tab from the List Box properties

19. By using the keyword **Bundle** before our load script section, we have embedded the images in our QlikView document.

20. Using the **Year** list box, repeat Steps 14 through 20.

21. View your results. They should look similar to the following image:

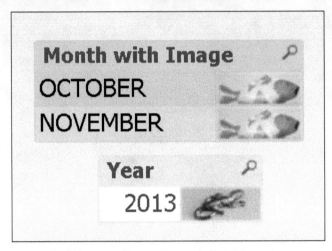

Figure 9-9: Month and Year list boxes with images

QlikView comes preloaded with some image files and sound files. These image and sound files can be used in your QlikView application directly, without loading them. We can refer to them within an expression or a file load script.

> See QlikView Help for a list of available images and sound files.

Summary

In this chapter, we have analyzed the CFO Example dashboard **Expenses** tab for ideas on expense reporting. We set our pie chart so that we could minimize and maximize it. We color-coded the legend key of the line chart, and we reviewed some simple formulas, similar to the ones that we used in the previous chapters, as a reminder, for creating legends that change when other data selections are made. We learned how to reference the columns of data in formulas. We also learned about creating links to files or web pages in our pivot table to extend the usefulness of a QlikView document. Additionally, we bundled our own image files into our QlikView document.

Next, we move on to the final chapter where we will learn to share our knowledge, gained through QlikView analysis, with others.

10
Sharing Your QlikView Insights

This final chapter discusses scaling up to an enterprise application with information on licensing, enterprise servers, data sources, mobile applications, QlikCommunity, the QlikView reference manual, and the latest addition to the QlikView offerings: **Qlik Sense**.

Sharing QlikView information with business associates

Perhaps you are the CFO of a company, and after downloading and investigating QlikView, you have decided that this is a tool that can really benefit your company. Or maybe you are a warehouse manager, an accounting analyst, or a sales manager, and you heard about QlikView from a friend. Now that you know what QlikView can do, you have recommended it to the upper management. The question they will most probably ask you is—What will it take? How do we make QlikView available for collaborative analysis in our company? The answer is: *Scale up to an enterprise application*.

Licensing and servers

Enterprise applications that are used to share data among multiple people require licensing on business servers from QlikView.

Licensing

Recall that the very first page when you open QlikView contains a link to the license information about the *Personal Edition* of QlikView. To open QlikView documents created by someone else, such as the one we created in *Chapter 1, Getting That Financial Data Into QlikView*, we would both need licenses. I would need a license so that the document could be saved for more than personal use, and you would need one to open a QlikView document (qvw) created by someone else.

QlikView Personal Edition can only open files created using that particular copy of QlikView. This means, with QlikView Personal Edition you cannot use your QlikView documents on different computers, you cannot share your QlikView documents with another unregistered user, or open a QlikView document from another user (exempted are documents specially prepared for personal use by QlikTech). This can be found on page 25 of the QlikView reference manual.

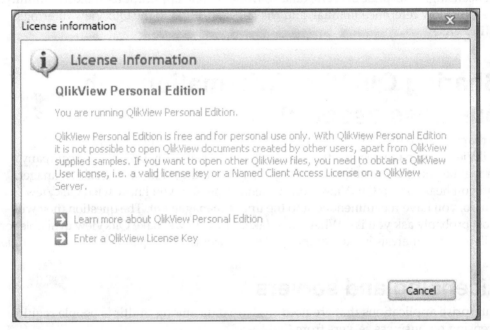

Figure 10-1: QlikView Personal Edition License information

Licenses are available for *named users* or as *concurrent user* licenses. Each QlikView licensed user has a fully functioning version of QlikView. When evaluating the cost of business intelligence software, the actual licensing costs are usually a small part of the return-on-investment calculation. QlikView is designed to help eliminate some of those extra service costs, often necessary with other business intelligence software, by helping you become your own developer.

The current pricing is available at the QlikView website. This is a good place to start when thinking about implementing an enterprise version of the software. The pricing information also includes information on the following:

- Maintenance and support
- Extra net solutions and services to make QlikView available outside your company's intranet firewall
- QlikView expressor – the IT management tool used for auditing usage, user security, and managing metadata such as dimension and formula consistency
- Training and services

Contact the QlikView sales department when you are ready for more information. Navigate to `http://www.qlik.com/us/explore/buy`, or use the **How to Buy** link on the Qlik website.

Figure 10-2: How to Buy link on the Qlik website

QlikView business servers

QlikView is a business, not a *not for profit foundation*, and it needs to make its profits from somewhere. QlikView expects that you will love the product and will recommend it to your company. The pricing model for enterprise licensing is comparatively reasonable, but you must remember to factor in the initial install and setup services that come with any new enterprise-level application. For this, QlikView offers their QlikView *Expert Services* with the *Foundation Services* offering, which are available at `http://www.qlikview.com/us/services/expert-services/foundation-services`.

A Foundation Services engagement will cover the following aspects:

- System architecture foundation
- Data architecture foundation

- Application architecture foundation
- Solution validation

You can connect to an enterprise server via the **Open in Server** command in the **File** menu, or from the **Open in Server** tab on the **Start** page.

Security, deployment, and technology in an enterprise application

By scaling up to an enterprise application, we are allowed to share information. An understanding of the interaction between the underlying technology and your current technology environment, along with how that can be used to deploy your licensed application while securing your information, is useful.

Security

When scaling up to an enterprise application, security of data becomes an issue. QlikView security can be integrated with Microsoft Active Directory, with **NTLM (Windows NT LAN Manager)**, and with third-party security (this requires QlikView Server Enterprise Edition). Further information on setting up security and integrating it with your environment is available when the license is purchased.

Deployment

To manage large deployments of QlikView, use the QlikView publisher component, which is an administrative interface for maintaining the QlikView analyses. QlikView publisher enables the reloading of data to a QlikView analysis on a periodic basis to ensure that the most current data is available. QlikView Publisher connects to the security directory servers within your organization, and applies the user security rules to the QlikView analysis to ensure appropriate user access. That way, if a user can see parts of the data but not all, he/she will have the correct secure access. QlikView publisher is licensed on a per-server basis and includes a separately licensable option for PDF report distribution capabilities.

Technology

QlikView is an in-memory BI pioneer using an inference engine that maintains associations in the data. Aggregations are calculated as needed for use by multiple people. QlikView caches the data in memory and uses proprietary technology to compress the data down to as much as 10 percent of its original size. The cached data helps optimize the power of the computer processor(s) for the fastest user experience possible.

The QlikView server component supports authentication and security models to ensure appropriate user access. Additionally, it supports concurrent access to the analyses by large user groups. QlikView server is designed to maximize the processing power of standard multi-core servers by spreading calculations over all the available CPU cores. The QlikView server can be deployed across more than one physical server into clusters to provide fault tolerance and additional scale.

For large enterprise deployments, multiple QlikView servers and QlikView publishers can be clustered to provide load balancing and fail-over capabilities.

QlikView publisher, QlikView Web parts for Microsoft SharePoint®, and QlikView Workbench are additional licensed modules of QlikView Server. QlikView Web parts for Microsoft SharePoint® and QlikView Workbench require the QlikView Server Enterprise Edition. Install them by purchasing and applying for a license to a QlikView Server. QlikView recommends that QlikView Server and Publisher reside on separate, dedicated server machines with no other applications running for the optimal performance of a QlikView deployment.

Data sources

The ability to bring in multiple sources of secure data is part of the underlying technology of enterprise applications. Out-of-the-box, QlikView can connect to **ODBC (Open DataBase Connectivity)** and **XML (eXtensible Markup Language)** data sources, as well as to Microsoft Excel. Developers can use the open **QVX (QlikView data exchange)** format for importing non-standard data sources into QlikView.

When you purchase an Enterprise Server license, in addition to the sources you could already connect to, you will receive connectors to the non-ODBC data sources, *Salesforce.com* and *Informatica*. There is an additional charge for the *SAP NetWeaver®* connector.

Mobile applications

The documents published on a QlikView Server can be accessed by different clients including the Internet Explorer plugin, AJAX Zero Footprint, and several mobile clients such as iPhone, iPad, Android, and Blackberry. It is now possible to distribute a QVW file to e-mail recipients defined in a field in the document. See QlikCommunity for tested devices and version details.

On mobile devices, users get a complete QlikView experience with interactive analysis and rich visualization. The mobile application is free to download and works with any QlikView 11 server license. Some of its important features are as follows:

- Delivery of the full QlikView business discovery experience across desktops, laptops, and mobile platforms
- Recognizing mobile devices and touch-enabling apps as needed
- Offering a single-object display mode on handheld devices for a more intuitive user experience

For more information about mobile device security for QlikView, download the document *DS-Technical-Brief-QlikView-on-Mobile-Security-EN.pdf* (by searching on Google).

Where to get further information

If any questions arise regarding QlikView, there is a wealth of resources to refer to including the QlikView website, QlikCommunity, and the PDF QlikView reference manual.

QlikCommunity

QlikCommunity is a discussion forum for QlikView users at `http://community. qlik.com/welcome`. Login with your QlikView ID, the same one you used to download the QlikView Personal Edition. Here, you will be able to set up your personal profile, join groups, ask questions, read blogs, and make suggestions for improvements to the QlikView functionality. The search function in the QlikCommunity website works well. If you are just starting out, chances are that you are not the only one to have ever run into the specific issue that you are facing.

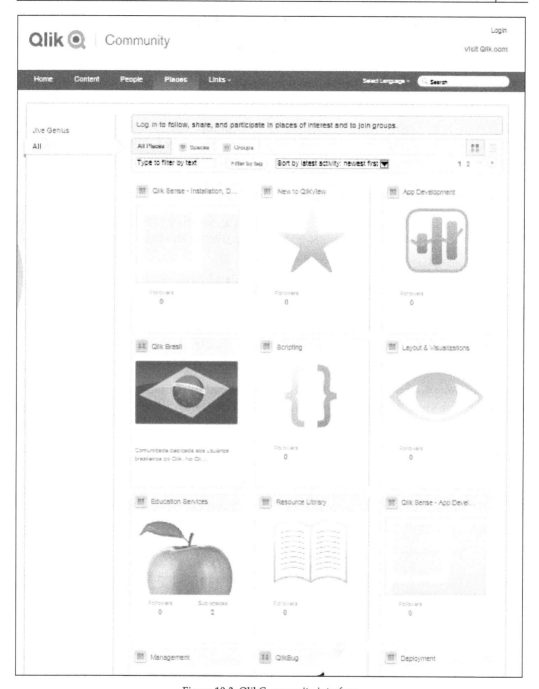

Figure 10-3: QlikCommunity interface

Development source control integration

With Qlikview 11, source control integration was introduced. This is the capability for the developers of QlikView documents to manage their work with source control tools. With these tools, developers can control and share their development efforts in a single QlikView QVW file.

This feature is available when using QlikView Desktop. An option in the **File** menu allows QlikView developers to connect a QlikView document to a source control system. More information on source control is available in a white paper at http://community.qlik.com. Find it by using the **Search** box in the website and limit your search to documents.

For more details on the Server requirements, check out the PDF document: *DS-QlikView-11-System-Requirements-EN.pdf* available on the QlikView website.

QlikView Reference Manual

When you installed QlikView, you also downloaded the *QlikView reference manual*. It is in the PDF format. To open it, navigate to C:\ProgramData\QlikTech\QlikView Documentation\Reference Manual. If you have Adobe Acrobat Reader installed, you can just double-click on the QlikView Reference Manual.pdf to open it.

In this document, you will find a wealth of additional information including the fact that older QlikView documents are compatible with the QlikView 11 Server and licensed clients.

 QlikView 7.52 and later share the same file format as QlikView 11. You can work in these versions in parallel virtually without giving it a second thought. The New QlikView 11 document features will, of course, not work in QlikView 7.52, 8, 9, or 10 but will be retained even if the document is opened and edited in an earlier version.

Figure 10-4: QlikView Reference Manual

Delving into Qlik Sense

Qlik Sense is the newest user interface in the QlikView family. It is similar to QlikView but designed to be implemented by an organization's technology department, gathering the data into server resources that are then accessed by the user community. It has much of the same data visualization and analysis application as QlikView. It allows business users to easily create personalized views, reports, and dashboards with drag-and-drop simplicity. Working with Qlik Sense is more like working with QlikView in WebView, which was not covered in this book. Like QlikVew, a sample application is available for download. The interface and the way it is used is more drag-and-drop than QlikView, but it also has a learning curve. It is more dependent upon conformed (formatted) data with less control in the loading process.

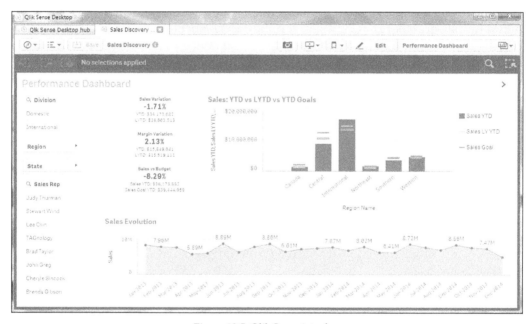

Figure 10-5: Qlik Sense interface

Summary

In this book, we have learned when to use QlikView along with many of the multiple features of QlikView. We have loaded data from Excel and learned about other data sources. We have experimented with performing analysis with QlikView in the section where we found the out of balance amount. We have modified the **Load Script**, loaded additional spreadsheets, and linked data.

We examined key performance indicators and learned about the different options available with QlikView to display them. We created the three most common financial KPIs and, during the process, learned about set expressions. We have created or modified most of the sheet objects available in QlikView in the preceding chapters, and created a common size income statement for analysis.

We have learned that dashboards should display key information in a quick-to-digest format, and that gauges, dials, and thermometers are often used incorrectly, causing confusion rather than clarification. We examined both the display choices and the underlying objects making up the multiple tabs of the QlikView CFO dashboard. The knowledge about the many sources of data that we can load into QlikView for analysis is very powerful. We can load information from files, database data sources, and from the Internet.

We found that there are many other sources for ideas to create a whole dashboard or just a tab that can be used for the type of analysis that best suits our business needs. We learned that our data sources are nearly limitless.

For the **Sales Analysis** tab of the CFO dashboard, we created a version better than the existing one by examining the existing version and the good and bad choices made in the display. We learned how to create a **Group** button to make more data available on a single display, without overcrowding or overloading information for the dashboard user.

- We created a new **Sales Analysis** dashboard tab using exactly the same data as in the original dashboard
- We learned how to create a toggle for rounding the numbers displayed so that they are easier to compare, and it is easier to remember how they compare for further investigation
- We rearranged and changed the original objects for a meaningful display
- We learned about containers and how to remove them and the objects inside
- We also created new containers and put objects in those containers

- We learned about the options for forecasting, trending, and the what-if analysis
- We examined the options for visualizing inventory turns and management
- We learned about the supply chain analysis options with the **Order Details** tab of the CFO dashboard
- Last, but not least, we examined the **AR Analysis** tab for ideas on reporting accounts receivable, aging for better cash flow planning, and collections management

In this final chapter, we covered the information required for taking QlikView to the next step, that is, as an enterprise analysis resource.

Enjoy!

Index

A

Asset Management dashboard
  about 55-57
  URL 55

C

CFO dashboard
  opening 37-39
  reopening 67, 85, 101, 113, 123
charts
  forecast lines, adding 86
  trend lines, adding 86
Chief Financial Officer (CFO) 37
colors, Trending dashboard
  about 90, 91
  formulas, experimenting with 91, 92
  layout themes 94
  obtaining 93
common size income statement
  about 30
  creating 31-36

D

data sources
  adding 58
  loading, from another QlikView
    document 59
  loading, from databases 64
  loading, from delimited files 64
  loading, from Excel files 63, 64
  loading, from files 59
  loading, from HTML files 62, 63
  loading, from QlikView files 60
  loading, from text files 64
  loading, from XML files 61
development source control integration
  about 144
  URL 144

E

enterprise application
  deployment 140
  securing 140
  security 140
  technology 141
Excel
  additional data, adding 9
  data, loading 5, 6
  multiple spreadsheet, loading 10-14
  order details dashboard, exporting 119
expenses dashboard
  bar chart formulas 130
  display, analyzing 124, 125
  formatting 131-135
  line chart, improving 127-129
  linking 131-135
  pie chart, minimizing 126
  pivot table variances, calculating 131
expression shortcuts 25, 26
eXtensible Markup Language (XML) 141

F

files
  data sources, loading 59
File Transfer Protocol (FTP) 64

Thank you for buying
QlikView for Finance

About Packt Publishing

Packt, pronounced 'packed', published its first book, *Mastering phpMyAdmin for Effective MySQL Management*, in April 2004, and subsequently continued to specialize in publishing highly focused books on specific technologies and solutions.

Our books and publications share the experiences of your fellow IT professionals in adapting and customizing today's systems, applications, and frameworks. Our solution-based books give you the knowledge and power to customize the software and technologies you're using to get the job done. Packt books are more specific and less general than the IT books you have seen in the past. Our unique business model allows us to bring you more focused information, giving you more of what you need to know, and less of what you don't.

Packt is a modern yet unique publishing company that focuses on producing quality, cutting-edge books for communities of developers, administrators, and newbies alike. For more information, please visit our website at www.packtpub.com.

About Packt Enterprise

In 2010, Packt launched two new brands, Packt Enterprise and Packt Open Source, in order to continue its focus on specialization. This book is part of the Packt Enterprise brand, home to books published on enterprise software – software created by major vendors, including (but not limited to) IBM, Microsoft, and Oracle, often for use in other corporations. Its titles will offer information relevant to a range of users of this software, including administrators, developers, architects, and end users.

Writing for Packt

We welcome all inquiries from people who are interested in authoring. Book proposals should be sent to author@packtpub.com. If your book idea is still at an early stage and you would like to discuss it first before writing a formal book proposal, then please contact us; one of our commissioning editors will get in touch with you.

We're not just looking for published authors; if you have strong technical skills but no writing experience, our experienced editors can help you develop a writing career, or simply get some additional reward for your expertise.

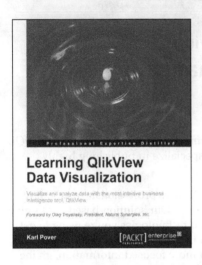

Learning QlikView Data Visualization

ISBN: 978-1-78217-989-4   Paperback: 156 pages

Visualize and analyze data with the most intuitive business intelligence tool, QlikView

1. Explore the basics of data discovery with QlikView.

2. Perform rank, trend, multivariate, distribution, correlation, geographical, and what-if analysis.

3. Deploy data visualization best practices for bar, line, scatterplot, heat map, tables, histogram, box plot, and geographical charts.

4. Communicate and monitor data using a dashboard.

Learning Qlik® Sense
The Official Guide

ISBN: 978-1-78217-335-9   Paperback: 230 pages

Get to grips with the vision of Qlik Sense for next generation business intelligence and data discovery

1. Get insider insight on Qlik Sense and its new approach to business intelligence.

2. Create your own Qlik Sense applications, and administer server architecture.

3. Explore practical demonstrations for utilizing Qlik Sense to discover data for sales, human resources, and more.

Please check **www.PacktPub.com** for information on our titles

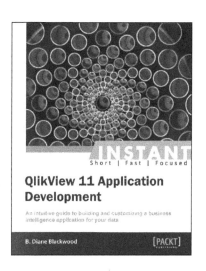

Instant QlikView 11 Application Development

ISBN: 978-1-84968-964-9   Paperback: 60 pages

An intuitive guide to building and customizing a business intelligence application for your data

1. Learn something new in an Instant! A short, fast, focused guide delivering immediate results.

2. Learn how to analyze data for business discovery with QlikView 11 with automatic data linking and wizards.

3. Create your own analysis interfaces using tables, lists, and charts.

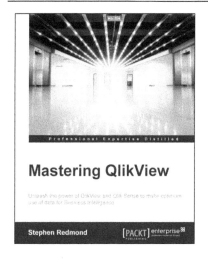

Mastering QlikView

ISBN: 978-1-78217-329-8   Paperback: 422 pages

Unleash the power of QlikView and Qlik Sense to make optimum use of data for Business Intelligence

1. Learn the best ways to load data to optimize the QlikView experience.

2. Display data in a way that is easy to understand for most number of users.

3. Discover advanced expressions and scripting techniques with lots of code and screenshots.

Please check **www.PacktPub.com** for information on our titles

www.ingramcontent.com/pod-product-compliance
Lightning Source LLC
Chambersburg PA
CBHW060137060326
40690CB00018B/3907